Set Adrift is the first book I would give to someone working through deconstructing their faith (or someone trying to help others who are deconstructing). John Marriott and Sean McDowell don't respond to the deconstruction phenomenon with alarmism or defensiveness. They invite questions and doubts and encourage a relentless search for truth. But they identify the guardrails and guides we need so that deconstruction ultimately results in a more authentic faith, rather than heresy or deconversion. *Set Adrift* is faithful to the Bible and historic Christian orthodoxy, balanced and reasonable in treating contested Christian doctrines, culturally insightful, and fair-minded to thoughtful objections. It is also not difficult to read and focuses on the most pressing interests readers are likely to bring to the table. If I could, I would give a copy of this book to every person engaged in the deconstruction conversation happening in the church today.

GAVIN ORTLUND, senior pastor of First Baptist Church of Ojai

If you or someone you know is questioning what they believe and why they believe it, *Set Adrift* is a must-read. This book insightfully outlines how a Christian struggling with doubt can properly deconstruct what they believe to experience an even stronger faith, while also exposing some of the most popular and dangerous worldviews attracting so many away from the Christian faith.

ALLEN PARR, author of *Misled* and founder of The Beat by Allen Parr

Here's a wise and helpful guide which demonstrates that deconstructing faith doesn't have to mean destruction of faith. Sean and John offer insights and practical experience that can help you follow Jesus more faithfully. This much-needed resource will help countless Christians pursue Christ. I'll be recommending this book for years to come!

LEE STROBEL, *New York Times* bestselling author and founder of The Lee Strobel Center at Colorado Christian University

T0006376

In the post-Christian West, most young Christians are going to, at some point, venture down a path of doubt and deconstruction. We can either throw up our hands in lament and resignation, or we can come alongside and equip them with tools of wisdom for their journey. *Set Adrift* takes the latter approach. Sean McDowell and John Marriott don't condescend to the reader who is in the process of deconstruction. They instead converse with them, offering understanding and empathy but also appropriate pushback, crucial considerations, and common pitfalls to avoid. I'd recommend this book to every Christian high school graduate. It may not stop some readers from questioning their faith, but I expect it will help many avoid losing it entirely.

BRETT MCCRACKEN, senior editor at The Gospel Coalition and author of *The Wisdom Pyramid*

SET ADRIFT

SET ADRIFT

Deconstructing What You Believe
Without Sinking Your Faith

Sean McDowell and John Marriott

ZONDERVAN
REFLECTIVE

ZONDERVAN REFLECTIVE

Set Adrift
Copyright © 2023 by Sean McDowell and Robert J. Marriott

Requests for information should be addressed to:
Zondervan, *3900 Sparks Dr. SE, Grand Rapids, Michigan 49546*

Zondervan titles may be purchased in bulk for educational, business, fundraising, or sales promotional use. For information, please email SpecialMarkets@Zondervan.com.

ISBN 978-0-310-14564-6 (softcover)
ISBN 978-0-310-14566-0 (audio)
ISBN 978-0-310-14565-3 (ebook)

Published in association with the literary agency of Mark Sweeney & Associates, Chicago, Illinois 60611.

Cover design: Charles Brock, Brock Book Design Co.
Cover photo: © Sata_Production / Adobe Stock
Interior design: Denise Froehlich

Printed in the United States of America

23 24 25 26 27 28 29 /TRM/ 10 9 8 7 6 5 4 3 2 1

*To Molly P. and all my
other students who've asked,
"Hey John, can we talk?"*
—JOHN

*To my father, for inviting my
questions and loving me through
my season of deconstruction.*
—SEAN

Contents

Introduction

We must pay the most careful attention,
therefore, to what we have heard,
so that we do not drift away.

—HEBREWS 2:1 (NIV)

"Hey professor, do you have office hours?"

There's nothing a professor likes more than when a student wants to meet and discuss something the professor taught in class. That day in my (John's) introduction to philosophy class, we had discussed the relationship between faith and doubt. Molly, a studio arts major, wanted clarification.

Or at least that's what I thought.

But when Molly and I met the following week, it wasn't the relationship between faith and doubt that was foremost on her mind.

"I was hoping we could talk about deconstructing my faith."

For the next hour, she shared with me her struggle identifying as a Christian. The problem wasn't so much that she was doubting the truth of Christianity as much as she was trying to determine what she thought Christianity is supposed to look like. More accurately, she was trying to understand why the evangelical tradition she identified with didn't reflect the values she saw as important to Jesus. How could she continue to be a Christian if her experience of Christianity was at odds with her most fundamental intuitions of Jesus's teachings?

Molly isn't alone when it comes to rethinking what it means to be a Christian. Across the United States, tens of thousands of young Christians serious about following Jesus are experiencing a crisis of faith. For some, the crisis is so great they never recover from it and eventually leave the faith. Molly didn't leave the faith, but she's one example of the many people who experience a faith crisis. We (Sean and I) have each had dozens of conversations with young people struggling deeply with their faith.

The number of Christians leaving the church and their faith is startling. Studies show that individuals are leaving the faith at significant rates and in significant numbers. For example, in 2018 the Pinetops Foundation estimated that roughly thirty-five million young people would leave the faith by 2050.[1] A previous and equally ominous study by the Pew Research Center maintained that for every person who becomes a Christian, four more leave the faith.[2] Many more studies could be cited, all of which lead to the same conclusion: college students and young adults are finding it increasingly difficult to retain their faith and, as a result, are deconverting from it.

Why are so many young Christians leaving the faith? While there are many reasons, a significant one is that they don't see any alternative. If the only choices are to live according to a Christianity they're at odds with or leave Christianity altogether, many opt for the latter. But there's another option instead of deconversion, and that's recognizing that there are other faithful ways to be a follower of Jesus than the Christian tradition inherited from one's family. Young

Christians begin looking for these "other faithful ways" when they realize the faith tradition they received as pure, unadulterated Christianity is actually an interpretation of what the Bible teaches, but not necessarily the only or even best one available. We think this realization is largely correct and even helpful. For a struggling believer, recognizing that there are other ways Christians throughout history have understood what faithfulness to Jesus looks like can help them pause the deconversion process. It can give them hope there's a home for them in the church universal, even if they no longer feel at home in their particular church community or tradition. This realization gives young Christians permission to rethink what an alternative expression of Christian faith might look like. In other words, it gives them the permission to deconstruct their faith.

Contrary to the way the word sounds, deconstruction in its contemporary usage is not necessarily *destruction*. In its common usage the term refers to the process by which something is disassembled, analyzed, and often reassembled in a new way.[3] Its purpose isn't necessarily to burn everything to the ground. Instead, its goal can be to rebuild a structure that's sturdier and more sensible than the previous one. Deconstructing Christians aren't necessarily skeptics; often they're seekers. They're not by definition dismissive of what the Bible teaches. On the contrary, for many, their commitment to taking the Bible seriously is what led to their sense of disillusionment with Christianity.[4]

Molly and tens of thousands of young Christians just like her are deconstructing their faith. They're asking if there are other ways to be authentically Christian than what they've experienced, and there are no signs of it stopping anytime soon. We can relate to Molly because we've both gone through the same painful process of rethinking what we believe.

Sean's Story

I remember the day my faith deconstruction began. It was in 1995, and I was a college student surfing the internet for the first time. I came across an atheist website dedicated to challenging the Christian claims about God, the Bible, and the historical Jesus.

To say I was unsettled is to put it mildly. Really smart people were challenging the ideas I was raised with. For the first time, I wondered if the Christian faith was true. Can I really trust the Bible as both accurate and inspired? What if Jesus didn't rise from the dead? Is evolution a better explanation than creation? These questions troubled both my mind and my heart.

Before this period in my life, my faith was something I took for granted. I have fond memories of attending Christian conferences, going on mission trips, and listening to my father as he taught the Bible. My parents raised me in the Christian faith. I can't remember ever *not* believing the Christian story about the world. Even though I certainly fell short of living it at times, the Christian faith made sense.

Yet when I was a college student, the answers I had based my faith on were no longer enough. Nagging doubts about my faith simply wouldn't go away. I remember staying up late at night reading the psalms of David as he wondered why God seemed absent in his time of need. Things no longer seemed black and white. Things were no longer simple.

As I wrestled with the big questions of life and wondered whether I could continue as a faithful follower of Jesus, I realized there was one person I needed to be honest with—my father. To understand how difficult this was for me, it's necessary to understand my dad's story as well.

To put it simply, my dad, Josh McDowell, has been one

of the most influential Christian leaders over the past half century. He has spoken to millions of young people and has sold tens of millions of books. He is probably best known for his books *Evidence That Demands a Verdict* and *More Than a Carpenter*, in which he documents the historical evidence that persuaded him to seriously consider the claims of Jesus.

He grew up in a small Michigan town in a deeply dysfunctional family. Sadly, my father can't remember his father (my grandfather) ever being sober until my father was in his twenties. He drank a couple of bottles of wine every day. My dad's older brother sued their father for everything, just out of spite; and one of his older sisters committed suicide. He was also severely sexually molested from the age of six until he was thirteen years old and finally strong enough to fight off the man who took advantage of him.

As you can imagine, my father was desperate for a life of happiness and meaning. He excelled as a student, made a lot of money by starting a painting company, was elected to student government, and yet nothing seemed to fill the void in his heart. After meeting some Christian students whose lives were markedly different than others, he decided to investigate the Bible and the historical resurrection to see if there was any validity to the claims of Christ. While there is much more to his story, the bottom line is that, through critically studying Christianity, he became convinced that Christianity was true and committed his entire life to defending it through books, speeches, and debates.

Can you see why my conversation with my father was so unnerving? How would he react to me deconstructing the faith he so deeply cherished and had been publicly defending for decades?

As we sat in a small café in the mountains of Breckenridge, Colorado, I told my dad about my doubts. His response took me by surprise. "I think it's great that you want to find truth," he said. "It's wise not to accept things just because you were told them. You need to find out for yourself if you think Christianity is true. You know that your mom and I love you regardless of what you conclude. Seek after truth, and take to heart the things your mom and I have taught you. And let me know if I can help along the way."

That is exactly what I needed to hear. He assured me of his love. And he showed confidence, not fear, as I began deconstructing my faith. We hope to communicate that same confidence and love to you.

Yet this wasn't just an intellectual journey for me. Although I was a pretty good kid growing up (I didn't do any of the "big" sins), I began to realize the depths of my own pride and rebellion against God. Like the older son in the story of the prodigal son, I was hardworking and dutiful but didn't understand God's love and acceptance (Luke 15:11–32). I had prided myself in being better than other people and didn't realize how blind I was to my own sinfulness. I too needed a savior.

As we will discuss in this book, doubt can be multifaceted. It can be intellectual but is also often emotional, moral, and relational. In my case, I had intellectual questions I needed to find answers for. I needed to be convinced of the truth of Christianity, but I also needed to become aware of my own sinfulness so I could personally experience God's grace in Christ.

John's Story

I remember the year, time, and place my deconstruction began. It was July 1987, midmorning, at a Bible camp in northern Ontario. I had volunteered to work at the camp as a cabin leader for the junior boys week. One of my responsibilities—other than being a cabin leader—was to run the camp games. My partner that week was Wes, a Bible college student and full-time staff member at the camp. Back then I was gung ho for Jesus but without much theological knowledge. I knew three things for sure. One, God loved everyone. Two, Jesus died to set people free from their sins. Three, people needed to hear that message. I went to the camp that week to share the gospel with those boys so they could be saved and experience the joy of knowing God. My faith was simple, sincere, and lacked any doubt. It was fantastic. What I lacked in theological depth I made up for in zeal and joy. I was eager to serve God in any way he wanted to use me. Whether that was as cabin leader or the cook's chore boy, it didn't matter to me. I was filled with joy that came from being certain I knew who God was and that he was good. But that was all about to change.

After the game we oversaw ended, and the campers had moved on to their next activity, Wes and I folded up the parachute we had used to play the game. As we did, I can't recall why, but the subject of God's sovereignty came up. It was a topic I, as a young believer, hadn't considered. Being a Bible college student, Wes took the time to enlighten me. He informed me about all the thorny issues surrounding the doctrines of election and predestination. As he did, it was like a bomb was dropped into my world, destroying my simple and sincere faith and the joy and security that accompanied it. First, Wes pointed out that the concept of divine sovereignty means that God ordains everything that happens. That made sense to me. To my way of thinking, God had to ordain everything, otherwise he couldn't be God. Wes then said something that shocked me. He maintained that if God does in fact ordain everything, then humans don't have free will. If we don't have free will, then the only people who believe in Jesus are those whom God ordained to believe in Jesus.

"Okay, what's the problem with that?" I asked. Wes reminded me that not everyone believes in Jesus, which means not everyone is chosen by God. Those not chosen by God spend eternity in hell. Not willing to accept that conclusion, I pushed back and argued that maybe we do have free will, to which he responded, "If humans have free will, then God is not in control of everything, and if God is not in control of everything, he is not God." When I finally understood what he was saying, nothing was ever the same again. Everything became complicated. I wasn't sure who God was or what I thought about him anymore. I can still recall the joy leaving my soul the moment I understood what Wes was saying.[5]

The paradox of divine sovereignty and human responsibility threw me into a tailspin. It set off a chain reaction of questions in my head. I questioned not only what I believed about God but also what I believed about Jesus, salvation, and even myself. My simple and naive faith had been shattered. It wouldn't be the last time I'd have a crisis of faith.

In 1997 I served at a homeless shelter in Hollywood called the Oasis. It was located one block north of the famous Hollywood Boulevard. Every Friday, I hung out with folks who were homeless. I met all sorts of characters during that time whom I still think about to this day, but none as much as a girl who called herself Knighty.

One Friday night we passed each other in the shelter. I had never seen her before. We made eye contact and I said, "Hello, how are you?" She was taken aback and replied with an angry tone, "What did you say?" I repeated myself and asked why she was so surprised I had spoken to her. "Look at me," she said, "no one speaks to me." I could see why. She was a mess of curly hair, ripped clothes, and a face tattoo. She was angry, defensive, and unwelcoming. Yet for some unknown reason, we hit it off, and so began a conversation that lasted for the next hour.

As we sat at a table in the dimly lit room, Knighty told me she was seventeen years old. She looked much older. Life on the streets had aged her noticeably. She said that for several years she bounced around the foster care system in the Midwest. During that time, she experienced every kind of abuse you can imagine. Desperate for change, she ran away and ended up, like many young people, on the streets of Hollywood. At the time we met, she was living in an abandoned lot under the 101 Freeway overpass.

It was hard to listen to her story. It was a heartbreaking journey. Many of the things she confided in me I can't write here because they are too disturbing. And Hollywood wasn't treating her any better. She was dirty, smelly, emotionally broken, and hopeless about her future. As she reached the end of her story of abuse and betrayal, I'll never forget what she said to me. Raising her head from the table and looking me in the eye, she paused and said, "Now is when you tell me that God loves me and has a wonderful plan for my life." What could I say? I was stunned speechless, and at that moment I myself wasn't sure if God really loved her. I finally muttered that I was sorry for everything that had happened and that even though I couldn't change it, I could be her friend going forward. To which she seemed slightly amused.

I asked if she would come back the next week so we could talk again. She told me she would come back the next week on one condition: if I promised I would be there. I promised. And with that she walked out into the night. I doubted I would ever see her again. Her life was so chaotic I suspected she might not even be in Hollywood by the time the next Friday rolled around. But just in case she did show up, I made sure to get to the shelter early the next week. I didn't want her to get there before me, not see me, and assume I wasn't coming.

When it came time for the shelter to open, I eagerly watched the door, looking for her. Within a minute or two, I saw her. She was staggering and in obvious pain. I walked over to ask her what was wrong. Between groans and gasps she told me what had happened. She said she had come back to the shelter to talk with me as she said she would. As she waited outside for the doors to open, a woman came up and started threatening her. She stood up to defend herself, yet the woman beat her. Knighty was punched and kicked until others broke up the fight. As it turned out, the woman who beat her was really a man dressed as a woman. Knighty never stood a chance. After she told me the story, she grabbed her stomach and said, "I need help. I think I just had a miscarriage." A female volunteer at the shelter took her to a clinic. That was the last time I saw her.

I vividly remember driving home from the shelter that night. I was furious at God. How could he have let this happen? After everything she had been through, why didn't God intervene? She was making her way to him. She was there that night to see me and to hear about him. The problem of evil had gone from being an academic and theoretical problem to a deeply personal, in-my-face problem. The difference was like night and day. I wasn't just troubled by the existence of both God and evil, I was angry at God. There was a rift in our relationship. I couldn't make sense of what I thought love to be and God's apparent lack of it. For the second time in my life, I was faced with the question of God's character. Was he really good? Did he really exist? If so, how could he account for himself? And how could I continue to love and serve him? After all, my compassion and concern for Knighty seemed greater than his. I struggled with those questions for a long, long time. The questions didn't dismantle my faith, but wrestling with them did reshape it. I'm still a Christian today, but my faith doesn't look quite the same as it did back then. And that's okay. Some things needed to change.

Tour Guide

If you can relate to Molly, and each of us, then this book is for you. Maybe your concerns are related to cultural issues, such as immigration, sexuality, or racial reconciliation. Perhaps yours are more like John's and are theological in nature. You wonder how a good God can command Joshua and the Israelites to annihilate the Canaanites. That doesn't seem very Jesus-like! Jesus told his followers to love their enemies, not to utterly destroy them. Or perhaps you feel a polarization between your church's values and the values you feel strongly about. You're convinced that love is love, regardless of whether it's between a man and a woman, or two men. But your church calls that sin. Quite possibly, given the growing insanity of our current political climate, you are turned off by the church's political involvement. Instead of seeing it as motivated by neighbor love, you think it looks more like a desire for power and control. Or maybe you've been hurt by the Christian tradition you were raised in and the trauma you've experienced has given you insight into the moral or theological problems with your faith community. Now you wonder if there are any faith communities that are healthy and safe, or if all expressions of Christianity suffer from the same deficiencies.[6] A deconstruction can begin in many ways. Everyone has a different issue that for them becomes the catalyst for rethinking what it means to be a Christian. What's important isn't how the process begins. What's important is how it ends: with a renewed faith, a heretical faith, or a lost faith.

What's the difference between a faith deconstruction that results in authentic Christianity and one that ends in heresy or deconversion? Two crucial factors make the difference: the *guide* we have and the *guardrails* we identify. What those wrestling with their faith need isn't so much to be told *what* to believe but rather *how* to believe. They need to know how to find their way back to faith, but not necessarily what that faith looks like in detail. They need to be given boundaries and then guidance for how to navigate within those boundaries. If the essence of Christianity is faithfulness to Jesus as Lord and King, then it's imperative that believers are free to reconstruct an expression of faith that they believe honors him. That doesn't mean a free-for-all. Each expression of faith needs to be within the boundaries mentioned in order to be genuinely Christian. That's where the guide comes in. This book is intended to be a practical aid in assisting you to rethink what you believe, helping you identify the boundary markers of an authentic Christian faith, and offering advice on how to maneuver within those boundaries as you reconstruct what you believe the Bible teaches.

Earlier we said that all Christian traditions are an interpretation of one sort or another. That's also true of our own perspective as authors. We have an understanding of Christianity that in some ways is unique to each of us. We are white males, each raised in the conservative evangelical tradition. We work at Biola University, a private Christian school in Southern California, and lean politically to the right on social and economic issues. And we acknowledge that those factors influence our understanding of Christianity. You too should keep in mind how those types of factors influence your beliefs.

But there is much more to our understanding of Christianity than our own unique life experiences. History plays an important role as well. Since the early days of the church, Christian leaders have written statements that capture the core of the faith, the essentials. If anyone's beliefs strayed beyond these essentials, the first Christians called them names like "heretic" and declared their belief unchristian. We would do well to take these creedal statements seriously. In an upcoming chapter we'll look at those statements and see how they provide the important guardrails needed to deconstruct faithfully.

That doesn't mean within those boundaries there isn't room for multiple understandings, different interpretations, and opposing views. There is! If those differing views are within the essential parameters of historical Christianity and believed out of sincere faithfulness to Jesus, they're legitimate for us to hold as Christians. That doesn't mean all our understandings will be correct. We should hold them humbly and in dialogue with others, always being willing to reevaluate and hold them up to scrutiny. We may even vehemently disagree with the interpretations of others, thinking they are in serious error and try to convince them of it. Sometimes our own theological beliefs will be wide of the mark. When that happens, we'll suffer consequences in line with our error. That's because living out of sync with reality tends to have negative effects. But if we affirm Jesus is Lord and construct our theology within the parameters established by the early Christians, there's room for differing approaches to following Jesus. There's room for *you* in the Christian community.

CHAPTER 1

Lost at Sea

And when the fog's over and the
stars and the moon come out at
night it'll be a beautiful sight.
—JACK KEROUAC

Imagine for a moment that you're standing on the shore looking out over the hypnotic pulse of ocean waves crashing on the beach. You feel the warmth of the sun on your skin, the sand between your toes, and the warm, salty ocean air on your face. In one hand you hold a paddle, and in the other your favorite paddleboard. This is your sweet spot. Every Sunday for as long as you can remember, you've launched out into the ocean from this very spot in search of a little "me time." You lie on your board, float over the breakers, and once clear of the surf you stand up and begin to paddle. It's a good day for paddleboarding: the ocean is calm, the sun is bright, and you can see for miles. And although you're now a quarter mile from the shore, you feel secure because you can still see the coastline and all the familiar landmarks that serve as reference points indicating where you are.

Suddenly, seemingly out of nowhere, a thick, dense fog engulfs you. None of the landmarks are visible. In fact, nothing is visible, not even your hand in front of your face. Your once enjoyable day out on the ocean is quickly turning into a nightmare. You're alone, drifting on the ocean without any bearings to help you navigate. A sense of disorientation sets in as you realize you're in real danger of being swept out to the open ocean. You must do something, but what? Which way do you paddle? Make the wrong decision and you may never return to the shore. You strain to see through the fog, thinking, "If only I could see a fixed point of reference, I could orient myself and know where the shore is." But they've all disappeared. You have no idea where you are or how to get back to shore. You're set adrift and at the mercy of the currents.

How did you feel as you imagined that scenario? We suspect, if you have a good imagination, you felt sheer panic at not knowing where you were, terror at the potential outcome, and an urgency to figure things out. Panic, terror, and urgency all resulted from the loss of a reference point. Not being able to see the shoreline, or anything else, created a crisis. Such is the power of reference points. We know where we are only in relation to things around us. We take them for granted, but when they disappear, we're literally lost without them.

Whether they're fixed objects we use for orientation in our physical world, or deeply held beliefs that structure our mental world, reference points give us our bearings. They tell us not only where we are but also who we are, where we belong, and what's important. They provide something we all crave: security. That's why when our most significant reference points—the beliefs we see as rock-solid truths that we orient our lives around—come into question, it can be as scary as being lost on the ocean in a dense fog. Panic, terror, and a sense of urgency can set in as we struggle to find our way back to the shore.

Who, Me?

If you're in the middle of rethinking your faith, then you know what we mean. You can *feel* the sense of urgency. Once you were a Christian on your paddleboard, floating on the sea of faith without a care in the world. The shore was clearly in view, and you could see all the familiar landmarks. You knew who you were and what you believed. Life was simple. It was black and white.

But for one reason or another, you've begun to question things. Doing so can feel just like being lost at sea. Feelings range from mild disorientation to debilitating emotional vertigo. You may even feel paralyzed. Questions can be directed at narrow parts of your faith, questioning specific doctrines and practices, or they may call into question the *entirety* of the Christian faith. Whichever the case, if the fog of doubt has settled around you, it's made the comfortable and familiar beliefs that dot the shoreline of faith, which once acted as your most certain reference points, impossible to see anymore. You might wonder if you even want to return to shore. Being in the fog long enough can cause you to doubt if the spot you left from is even worth returning to. Maybe there's a better one further up the coast that is more intellectually and emotionally satisfying.

As professors at a Christian university, we often walk with students through this painful, difficult process. Raised in the church and committed followers of Jesus, they come to college wanting to be educated and trained to make a difference in the world for the Lord. While some know the Bible well, many are zealous but lack such knowledge. Many have never read the entire Bible or possess much depth beyond a cursory knowledge of basic Christian doctrine. Over the next four years, as they intellectually come of age, they're exposed to new aspects of the Bible and historic Christian teachings. They frequently encounter various kinds of beliefs or teachings that offend them. Some are *theological issues* like the Trinity or predestination. Can we really understand these doctrines, or do we have to live in uncertainty? Others are offended by *moral issues* like genocide, slavery, or misogyny that the Bible seems to promote. Does the Bible honestly endorse these things? Seeming *logical issues*, like contradictions, errors, or mistakes in Scripture, plague many. Can we really trust that the Bible is reliable? They know they are drawn to the person of Jesus, but they're increasingly unsure they love the religion that bears his name, or at least the version of it they've been raised in.

So begins the process of weighing and evaluating the claims they've inherited from their family, their church, and their university professors to determine which ones they can affirm and which ones they can't. If you're reading this book, we suspect it's because, at least to some degree, like many of our students, you are rethinking your faith. Or you see many of your peers caught somewhere between wanting to be Christian and unsure of whether they can be. Today, there's a popular word for this process: *deconstruction*. Understanding the background of this word will help bring some clarity to your own personal journey and to the larger cultural movement that goes by its name.

Defining Deconstruction

Technically speaking, *deconstruction* is the term given to a particular kind of philosophical and literary analysis. The expression was coined by French philosopher Jacques Derrida and, as the term implies, is a strategy for undoing or taking apart claims that maintain to have discovered *the* true meaning of a text, written or otherwise.[1] Derrida attempted to do this by showing that all knowledge claims are based on wrong assumptions and incoherent concepts.[2] To accomplish this, he analyzed interpretations of various texts and philosophical systems—which claimed to represent reality—to show that if one looks close enough, such claims self-destruct. Derrida's motive in deconstructing knowledge claims arose from his concern over illegitimate appeals to authority and exercises of power. The belief that one has reached the single, correct interpretation of reality provides a great excuse for condemning those who disagree with it. Those people then become marginalized, excluded, and oppressed. But if the "official" interpretation of a matter can be shown not to reflect reality but to be only a social construction, then it loses its power to oppress. By destabilizing truth claims, Derrida made space for a range of alternative interpretations. In short, deconstruction undermines knowledge about reality. All truth claims become collective hunches. As a result, none should be privileged to the exclusion of others.

On the surface, deconstruction's desire to create space for competing interpretations so that no one is excluded sounds noble. Indeed, all people deserve to be loved and accepted for who they are. No one should be oppressed. But there are other ways to make sure of that without embracing this kind of deconstruction.[3] The cost of following Derrida down that rabbit hole is too high, leading to the dead end of radical relativism, where all interpretations of reality are equally unwarranted.[4] Furthermore, if Derrida was correct, then the Bible's claim to be a word from God is no more authoritative than any other claim about reality.[5] For those reasons and more, we reject Derrida's version of deconstruction.

Another approach to deconstruction is rooted in the rejection of evangelical faith. Proponents encourage Christians to deconstruct their faith because it is—by virtue of being an evangelical—complicit with injustice, oppression, and toxic religiosity. Now, we agree that if one's faith has inherent aspects of toxic religiosity, they ought to be purged. But often what is considered toxic religiosity is any belief or practice that doesn't align with what is currently considered socially progressive. We also reject this version of deconstruction. And we think you should too.

Naturally, given the original meaning of the word *deconstruction*, and the way it is marketed online by some sources, it's understandable why some Christians don't like using it to describe the process of faith revaluation.[6] We're sympathetic to their concerns. Yet we suspect that very few Christians who say they're deconstructing their faith have heard of, much less read, Derrida. Rather, they're becoming intellectually self-aware. For many, deconstruction results from conceptually stepping outside their faith for the first time and looking back on it with a critical eye. Instead of being an actor in the play, they find themselves the critic in the audience, wondering if the version of the play they're watching is reflective of what the playwright envisioned.

This shift from actor to critic often results from, among other things, encountering Christians who have different theological, scientific, political, or moral views; being hurt by fellow Christians; feeling that one's Christianity is at odds with the moral sensibilities of the surrounding culture; or reading Scripture and seeing it at odds with one's personal experience. When that happens, some reflexively find themselves asking, as we both did, "Why do I believe that what my church has taught me reflects what Jesus wants?" to which they answer, "Perhaps I should look into this, because I'm becoming suspicious of the version of Christianity I've been handed and told to believe." Thus begins the process of deconstruction. This is how we both felt for a season.

When we speak of deconstruction, what we're talking about isn't much different from the process of "reforming" what one believes. So why not use the term *reforming* for this book? Because that's not the word that many young people use to describe what they're experiencing today. They speak of deconstructing, not reforming, rethinking, or reevaluating. So, following the apostle Paul, we've chosen to become all things to all people so that, by all possible means, we might communicate effectively.

To put our cards on the table, we suspect that most young Christians who are deconstructing their faith aren't doing it just so they can show it to be an inherently imperialistic, intolerant, oppressive ideology that they're justified in leaving behind. On the contrary, we believe that large numbers of those who identify as deconstructors do so because they desire to follow Jesus more faithfully. They want to know truth. Thus, we want to be helpful guides to encourage them along their journey. If that means using their language, then we are happy to do so. When we use the term *deconstruction* in a positive way in this book, we mean the following: a process of analysis that Christians who want to follow Jesus engage in because they "doubt the faith they've received is the fully refined good that God intends, and are seeking to sift out the dross and keep what is most precious."[7]

In the coming chapters, this is the definition we intend in using the term *deconstruction*.

How to Deconstruct Well

It's fair to say that young Christians today are more prone to rethinking their faith than previous generations. We'll address why this may be in chapter 6, but for now we want to state an obvious reason why many young Christians deconstruct their faith: They've inherited a set of beliefs and practices they no longer feel comfortable identifying with. They have doubts about the faith that has been passed on to them. So they're pulling the system apart, laying the parts on the table, evaluating them piece by piece, and (hopefully) putting them back together in ways they believe better reflect how a Jesus follower should live and believe. Deconstruction can be a good thing when it is motivated by faithfulness to Jesus.

As you can imagine, deconstructing your faith can raise concerns for other Christians, typically older ones. It's not necessarily because they're old, or they're closed-minded fundamentalists, or they don't truly care about you. That might be the case for some, but most are concerned because the fog cuts both ways. While you're out on the ocean unable to see the shore, they're on the shore, scared because they can't see you. They aren't sure if you're heading back to shore or further out to sea. As you go through this process, please keep something in mind: *having a loved one rethink something as important as their religious beliefs can produce a lot of anxiety in those on the shore, because neither of you know whether you will come back.*

I (Sean) shared earlier about how my father responded to my doubts. He is truly an optimist who sees the "glass" as 99 percent full. But understandably, my mom responded differently. She's a realist. And, of course, she is my *mother.* It hurt my mom personally that I questioned the faith I was raised in. She was deeply concerned and wondered if she had somehow failed as a parent. I didn't understand the depth of her distress at the time, but now that I'm a parent, I see exactly why she felt that way. She felt my pain as only a parent can. We mention this not to put a burden on you but to encourage you to be aware of how others may process your deconstruction. Like my mom, some may respond with concern.

Others might be dismissive. Because some Christians who deconstruct their faith don't return to shore, it can be easy for those on the shore to assume that those in the fog are arrogant rebels. We often hear comments like, "Who are these people to think they can reinterpret what the Bible clearly teaches? They're just looking for loopholes to believe what they want!" Perhaps that's true of some folks going through deconstruction. For them, deconstruction is a means by which they can justify rejecting the parts of the Bible they don't like or the Christian faith altogether. It's not hard to find such people since the teaching of the Bible often cuts against the grain of our desires. As Paul said, the cross is foolishness to some and a stumbling block to others (1 Cor. 1:23). But that's not necessarily what's happening with all or maybe even most young Christians asking hard questions. For them, it's not arrogance or rebellion that drives deconstruction. Rather, it's a desire to know and live the truth. Far from not caring what the Bible teaches or avoiding difficult passages, many deconstructing Christians do so out of a desire to be biblical. Yet, for various reasons, they are unsettled by the version of Christianity they've inherited.

Who This Book Is For

If you see yourself in the description in the previous section, then this book is for you. We hope that as you wrestle with your faith, we can be practical guides to help you do so in a wise and faith-building manner. We also hope your wrestling results in a faithful deconstruction, one that leads you back to the shore.

However, you should know up front that we aren't going to

tell you what type of Christian you *should* be. We're not trying to get you back to the same spot on the shore you left from. Our hope is not that you become *this* type or *that* type of Christian. Our desire is to help you find a way to be a faithful disciple of King Jesus, and we don't expect that it's likely you'll return to the same place you left from. That's okay. The shoreline of Christianity is long and has a range of landing spots. It's populated by communities that share core beliefs but also have different theological systems and ways of practicing those beliefs in community. They have varying perspectives on what shore life looks, sounds, and feels like. Some of those communities are very old and have well-established rhythms of life because they've been on the shoreline for hundreds of years. Others are of a more recent vintage with a more contemporary feel. But though they may be on different stretches of the beach, they share the same shoreline. It's less important which specific Christian community you join than what your relationship to Jesus is like and that you join *some* Christian community. Each of the communities on the shoreline have positives and negatives. They don't share all the same beliefs or interpretations about shore life, but on the ones that matter, they do.

You might have to examine multiple communities and traditions to find one you think best represents what Jesus calls his people to believe and do. Once you find one, if you spend enough time there, as in any Christian community, you'll likely become disappointed. That's because none of them exactly mirror the way of living and believing laid out in the Bible. They are made up of sinful, fallen people (like us and you). But given the length of the shoreline and the many communities that populate it, we're convinced that if you want to follow Jesus, you'll find one that's both *faithful* to him and *a fit* for you.

This book is intended to help you navigate your way back to the shore when you're adrift in the fog of deconstruction. It's a practical guide that offers suggestions for what to do when you're not sure what you believe anymore. The target audience is people who want to follow Jesus. These are Christians who don't intend to deconvert and leave the faith but feel deeply unsatisfied with the kind of Christianity they've experienced and wonder if there is another way to be a Christian. They may have a lot of questions and doubts about Christian faith and practice but still want to follow Jesus.

We recognize that some of you unless you can find another way of being Christian, will end up leaving the faith entirely. Why is that? Because you'll eventually conclude that regardless of which community of faith you return to, all of them affirm beliefs and values you find objectionable. This would be proof for you that Christianity is either untrue or, if true, unworthy of allegiance. In either case, you'd no longer be paddling around in the fog of doubt. You will have found your way out. However, you'd have done so by paddling further out to sea, away from the shoreline of Christianity and all its various communities. You may not know which shore you will eventually arrive at, but you'd be sure of which one you have left behind. Your faith in Jesus will have sunk.

Who This Book May Not Be For

We want to say this up front: if you're at the point in your deconstruction in which the truth of Christianity is on the table, then this book isn't designed specifically for you. If you're questioning the existence of God and the basic claims the Bible makes about the life, death, and resurrection of Jesus, this book will not help you find answers to those specific questions. We suggest you begin with *Evidence That Demands a*

Verdict, which I (Sean) wrote with my father. But we do think you will find this book helpful, nonetheless. It can help you reflect on the decisions you've made in your own journey so you can think carefully about what it means to follow (or consider following) Jesus. If you are thinking about leaving your faith entirely, we obviously can't stop you, but this book can help you examine the steps of your own faith journey in a careful, systematic, thoughtful way. We see many young Christians reject their faith in knee-jerk fashion, based entirely on their limited experience. We hope this won't be you.

As you'll see in a following chapter, we each have wrestled with the big questions about Jesus and the Bible, and we personally know how unsettling such a process can be. "What if I lose my faith?" "Lose my community and friends?" "Lose my identity?" Is there anything in life more important than these things? If so, we can't think of them. So if this is where you are, we feel you. Please know we have been there. And we have addressed these questions in this book, but we won't be making the positive case for Christianity. This is not an apologetics book. This book is a guide designed primarily for those whose deconstruction journey has progressed to the place where they believe the claims of Jesus are true but who are largely dissatisfied with the version or take on Christianity they were born (or born again) into. It is for Christians looking for a wise way to follow Jesus amid their doubts, questions, and uncertainties. It's for people who are wondering if their inherited version of Christianity is the only game in town or if there are other ways of being Christian that seem to better align with their understanding of what Jesus calls his people to. In short, this is a book for those trying to determine *the way* of Jesus, not if Jesus is *the Way*. If that's you, we invite you to keep reading.[8]

Reflection Questions

1. Have you related to the paddleboarder at any point in your faith journey? In terms of your faith now, are you sailing on calm and clear seas, sensing the fog set in, or feeling engulfed by it?

2. We mentioned three types of deconstruction. Which of these is most common among those you know?

3. Do you agree that young Christians today are more prone to deconstruct than previous generations? Why or why not?

4. Is it possible that your deconstruction is really a pretense to justify letting go of aspects of the faith you dislike? If so, what might they be? Are any other "hidden" motivations involved?

5. If you are in a season of deconstruction, have you told those around you? How did they respond? If not, how might they respond?

CHAPTER 2

Delights and Dangers

Whenever we give up, leave behind,
and forget too much, there is always
the danger that the things we have
neglected will return with added force.
—CARL JUNG

Delight yourself in the LORD,
    and he will give you the desires of your heart.
—PSALM 37:4

In one of the greatest physical feats in human history, climber Alex Honnold summitted El Capitan, a sheer granite rock face rising over three thousand feet from the canyon floor of Yosemite National Park. What made Honnold's achievement so remarkable wasn't that he was the first to climb the iconic rock formation—many had done so before him. Rather, he rocketed to legend status because he climbed it without any safety equipment! That's right, he climbed three thousand feet with only his hands and feet gripping the smallest of cracks and crevices to keep him from falling; and falling was a very real possibility.

Over thirty climbers *using safety equipment* have fallen to their deaths trying to ascend El Capitan. That raises the question, If climbing El Capitan is so dangerous, why do people risk it? One reason is that there's something exhilarating about facing danger. When the stakes are high and you win, the payoff can make the risk worth it. But when you face danger, failure is always a genuine possibility.

While deconstructing one's faith isn't the same kind of danger as climbing El Capitan, there are similarities. Both have potential upsides and terrifying downsides. Climbing El Cap can give you a major adrenaline rush, increase your self-esteem, and make you a living legend among your friends and the climbing community—but the risk is incredibly high. You can lose your life. In a similar way, deconstructing can have a lot of upsides, but it carries great risk. If Christianity is true, the danger of deconstructing unwisely, and without proper support, is even greater than the danger of scaling iconic granite walls. In this chapter we'll look at the benefits and the risks of deconstruction. In doing so, we hope to help you experience the delights and avoid the dangers.

Delight

In my midtwenties, I (John) worked as a maintenance man for an old, rundown mom-and-pop motel in my hometown. Part of my job consisted of renovating the dilapidated, 1970s-style rooms. I replaced the drywall, changed the carpet, replaced the furniture, retiled the bathrooms, and painted the walls and ceilings. It was a lot of work, but it needed to be done if they wanted anyone to stay there. But as difficult and time consuming as the work was, it was also enjoyable. I knew that, with each coat of paint and newly installed toilet, I was creating a space that people would enjoy. The combination of tearing down the old and creating something beautiful made the work gratifying.

Like old motel rooms, some expressions of the Christian faith have problems and need renovation too. If those problems aren't addressed, it's hard to imagine why a person would stay in that faith any more than a person would stay in a grungy motel room. However, when those problems are addressed, the newly gained benefits change one's faith from something to endure to something to enjoy. We can think of three benefits of deconstruction that can do just that.

1. A HEALTHIER FAITH

The word *toxic* is used a lot today. There are toxic substances, toxic waste, and toxic relationships, just to name a few. Something becomes toxic when it's been poisoned to such a degree that it can be debilitating or deadly. Can Christianity be toxic? Sadly, yes. Certain expressions of Christianity can be toxic, and believers caught within them are wise to deconstruct. For example, some versions of Christianity are characterized by hostility, anger, and judgmentalism. Consider the painful words Mark Karris heard at a men's conference:

> The famous Pentecostal giant, T. F. Tenney, was the guest speaker. As he railed about the need for holiness codes for the church, he shouted a line I will never forget. Talking about Christians smoking cigarettes, screaming at the top of his lungs, he proclaimed,
> "If they are smokin' now, they will be smokin' later!"
> The whole crowd was energetically and excitedly cheering and yelling, "Amen! Praise God! Praise the Lord!!"
> It was as if time stood still. I just started weeping. With

tears down my face, I thought to myself, "How could these people celebrate and jump up for joy that fellow brothers and sisters who smoke cigarettes will be going to Hell and be tortured for eternity?"

The dissonance in that moment was something I never forgot. And, it was in that precise moment I knew that whatever was going on here, was not of love, and was a tribe I could never call home again.

In that day, the seeds of deconstruction were sown.[1]

Mark's experience is not an isolated one. We've spoken with dozens of Christians who tell similar stories. And for them, their experiences also sowed "the seeds of deconstruction."

It's not always a harsh version of Christianity that pushes believers out of the faith. For some it's the relationship between the church and politics. Sadly, some Christians, on both sides of the political aisle, have sold Jesus out for raw political power. Others have become disillusioned because of an authoritarian leadership style that was spiritually abusive. Recently some of evangelicalism's most well-known leaders have been removed from their roles in ministry over allegations of spiritual abuse.[2] Without question there are toxic expressions of the faith that need to be deconstructed, and doing so can result in a healthier and more biblical faith.

2. A GENUINE FAITH

It's sometimes said that God has no grandchildren, which is shorthand for the claim that to have a relationship with God, each person must individually choose to become his child. No one gets into the family of God because of the faith of their parents. We take that to be a solid biblical truth. To have a relationship with God, each of us needs to take responsibility for our own rebellion and to trust in Jesus as the one who paid for our sins. Becoming a Christian is much more than simply believing the right things. After all, even the demons have good theology (see James 2:19). Saving faith involves personally submitting to Jesus as Lord and intending to follow him. That's what the Bible means when it says, "Believe in the Lord Jesus, and you will be saved" (Acts 16:31).

In turn, that means each believer is responsible to learn what it is that their Lord wants from them. Each of us has a duty to study Scripture to learn how God wants us to live. In saying this, we are not advocating for an individualistic, "anything goes" approach to the Bible. As we will explain in chapter 4, some established boundaries need to be honored as we approach Scripture. At the same time, though, Jesus is clear: we are to love the Lord our God with all our hearts, souls, and minds (Matt. 22:37). We are to be like the Bereans, who examined Scripture daily to discover truth (Acts 17:11). God expects us to think hard about his Word, do our best to understand what it teaches, and then live it out. In doing so, our faith becomes more genuine than when we merely uncritically accept the dogma that has been handed down to us.

3. A TRUTHFUL FAITH

Like many who have seen a Christmas play, we used to believe Jesus was born in a stable behind the local hotel. We also took it for granted that the wise men showed up the night he was born. After all, they appeared in all the Christmas plays. We no longer believe either of those things. Why? Because we took the time to investigate those beliefs and compare them with what the Bible says. What we found was a big surprise! It turns out Jesus probably wasn't born in a stable because the local hotel was full. More likely, Jesus was born in the house of one of his relatives and placed in a feeding trough because there wasn't room for Mary and Joseph in the lodging place of the home.[3]

When speaking on the importance of truth, I (Sean) often ask audiences to close their eyes and point in the direction they think is north. Then, with their hands still extended, I ask people to open their eyes. Inevitably, people point nearly every direction possible, which often elicits laughter from the audience (without fail, someone always points straight up). People quickly understand that truth matters when we travel. If you are in Texas, for instance, and trying to go north to Oklahoma, you could end up in New Mexico, Louisiana, or Mexico if you have faulty directions. But if you have a GPS, which puts you in touch with reality, you can navigate to your destination smoothly.

Here's the key idea: *truth has consequences*. This is the case for driving, and it is also the case for faith. It was a bit disappointing to discover that our cherished views of Christmas were probably wrong. Admittedly, being wrong about the minor details of the Christmas story is pretty inconsequential. But many other beliefs we hold are very consequential. For instance, what is true love? If we don't understand the nature of love, how can we properly love God and love our neighbors? If we don't understand truth, then how can we rightly worship God in truth (John 4:24)? Views we hold about the proper use of money, the nature of spiritual gifts, the character of God, and God's design for marriage have *big* implications for how we live. Deconstruction can spur us to embrace true beliefs and shed false ones so we can live a more truthful faith.

Dangers Ahead

Renovating a motel room has many positive benefits but also some potential drawbacks. For one, it can be dangerous. Power tools can cut off fingers. Standing on ladders comes with the possibility of falling off them. Basements flood and require pumping. Electrical panels break and need fixing. One misstep can be costly. In the same way, deconstruction also has dangers. The most concerning is that deconstructing can result in a paradigm shift that leaves you either a heretic or an apostate. The goal of deconstruction, as we have defined it, is to stay faithful to Jesus and not to abandon one's faith. But deconversion is a genuine possibility when wrestling with key facets of the faith. If a paradigm shift is that dangerous, it raises the questions, What are paradigms and how do they shift?

Paradigm Shift

A paradigm is a framework or set of beliefs we use to make sense of reality. One can think of it as a mental model of how one understands the world to be. Each of us has a paradigm—sometimes called a worldview—but we're often unaware of it. We see reality by way of our paradigms, but we don't *see* our paradigms. Although it is not a perfect analogy, a paradigm is somewhat like a pair of glasses. We see *through* the glasses to the world but often forget we are wearing them. Only when an aspect of reality comes along that doesn't fit within our paradigm does it rise to the level of our consciousness. Think of it like a crack in our glasses.

It's important to point out that not all beliefs in a paradigm are of equal importance. Some beliefs are primary and others secondary. *Primary beliefs* are those at the center of the paradigm, the foundational "truths" that can't be given up without the paradigm collapsing. For example, if a Christian concluded that God did not exist, then their Christian paradigm would collapse since the existence of God is a primary belief of the paradigm.

On the other hand, *secondary beliefs* are assumptions that naturally, but don't necessarily, follow from the core beliefs.

In other words, if the primary beliefs are true, then the secondary beliefs are likely true as well. Unlike primary beliefs, secondary beliefs can be adjusted and even discarded to save the primary beliefs if contrary evidence seems to require it. Returning to the previous example, a Christian coming to believe in evolution has different implications for the Christian paradigm than rejecting belief in God. Assuming we are not referring to a purely materialistic account of human origins, the Christian can change their interpretation of the first two chapters of Genesis to allow for evolution. By sacrificing a secondary belief in a literal creation account, a Christian can potentially save the paradigm and their faith.[4] Although changing secondary beliefs doesn't mean the paradigm will necessarily collapse, if too many secondary beliefs must be changed to save the primary beliefs, the paradigm then becomes vulnerable. Why? Because even though the primary beliefs don't entail the secondary beliefs, they are consistent with them. If Christians adapt too many secondary beliefs, they may justly be accused of performing "mental gymnastics" to save the narrative.

The foundational role paradigms play in our understanding of the world and ourselves means they give us a significant sense of security. Changing our paradigm means changing our view of the world, which can be traumatic. That's why when contradictory data challenges our paradigm, one natural response is to dismiss the data. If we can explain away the counterevidence, we can alleviate the cognitive dissonance we feel and go on maintaining our beliefs with seeming intellectual integrity. Yet no matter how much we may want to retain our paradigm, if we're faced with mounting conflicting data, we may be forced to reconsider our core beliefs. Here's the bottom line: when we are confronted with evidence that challenges our paradigm, we can reject the evidence with counterevidence or revise our paradigm. To use the earlier metaphor, we can either ignore a crack in our glasses or buy an entirely new pair.

Paradigm(s) Shift

A person experiences a paradigm shift when they encounter too many phenomena that no longer fit with how they see the world. They experience puzzle pieces that simply won't fit. Some people experience paradigm shifts over a long period of time, which usually involves a journey of taking one step forward and two steps back until they exhaust the reasons they had for affirming their beliefs. Others have a more decisive experience in which they reject their former paradigm more suddenly. At that moment, the paradigm collapses and another takes its place.

Why have we spent so much time explaining both paradigms and paradigm shifts? Here's why: deconstruction can degenerate into a paradigm shift. Why is that a problem? Paradigm shifts lead to either heresy or apostasy. Therefore, it's vital to understand the nature of paradigms and how they can change as you deconstruct what you believe. As we've seen, deconstruction can have some delightful results, but it can have some dangerous ones too. It's to those we now turn.

Danger 1: Deconversion

Bart Campolo is a former urban missionary and youth worker. I (Sean) remember hearing him speak at Biola when I was an undergrad. Over lunch, he encouraged me to consider serving in the inner city. So, after college, I spent a year working at the Dream Center in Los Angeles. It was an amazing year of being stretched in my faith, interacting with people from various ethnic backgrounds, and learning to serve others. Bart has been a friend for many years. Now he is a *former* Christian. It broke my heart when I first heard of his deconversion—and it still does.

Bart's deconversion from the faith was big news in 2014 because he is the son of Tony Campolo, one of evangelical Christianity's biggest names in the 1980s and 90s. What was it that caused Bart to lose his faith? Well, it wasn't one thing, and it didn't happen overnight. He has described his faith as passing "through every stage of heresy."[5] Bart slowly deconstructed what he believed until there wasn't anything left. He began by adjusting his secondary beliefs to match up with the reality he saw around him. Eventually, however, no amount of adjusting could protect the primary beliefs of his Christian faith.

For Bart, it started with his exposure to poverty and crime. He couldn't reconcile the despair of those he was ministering to with God being all-loving and all-powerful. If God really was loving (a primary belief for Bart), why were those he ministered to experiencing such hardship? Didn't God love them? In particular, he was troubled by the rape of a young girl in the inner city. Such evil and pain weighed against Bart's belief that God was all-loving. But in the face of this evidence, he didn't reject his Christian paradigm. He did what we all do when we encounter counterevidence to our paradigm—he adjusted one of his secondary beliefs. The belief he adjusted was that God is all-powerful. Bart reasoned that if God loved people, he would want to end poverty, and if God was all-powerful, he *would* end poverty. Since people were suffering under extreme destitution, it must be because God was either not loving or not powerful. Bart chose to believe God had to be loving, which left the only option available to him—to deny that God was all-powerful. Limiting God's sovereignty allowed him to maintain his belief in the goodness of God and thus one primary belief of his Christian paradigm.[6]

Many would argue that God being all-powerful *is* a primary belief of the Christian paradigm and to relinquish it would cause the Christian paradigm to collapse. It seems that, in hindsight, Bart would agree. With the benefit of having a few years to reflect on his deconversion, he said that changing his view on God's sovereignty "was the beginning of the end."[7] Why?

> Because once you start adjusting your theology to match up to the reality you see in front of you, it's an infinite progression. So, over the course of the next 30 years . . . my ability to believe in a supernatural narrative or a God who intervenes and does anything died a death of a thousand unanswered prayers.[8]

Campolo's theological accommodation didn't stop at rethinking the nature of God. It resulted in him questioning and ultimately rejecting the authority of the Bible.

> For a while I struggled to reconcile the Bible's clear injunctions against homosexual behavior with my dawning realization that my gay friends' sexual orientations were no more chosen than my own. In the end, however, none of my interpretive "solutions" truly satisfied both my friends and my evangelical sensibilities, and I knew I had to choose between them.[9]

Faced with the choice to believe that "the Bible's clear injunctions against homosexual behavior" were right or that his friends' behavior was loving, Bart chose his friends. He continued with one theological accommodation after another.

I passed through every stage of heresy. It starts out with sovereignty goes, then biblical authority goes, then I'm a universalist, now I'm marrying gay people. Pretty soon I don't actually believe Jesus actually rose from the dead in a bodily way.[10]

Eventually, in his words, "there was literally nothing left of my evangelical orthodoxy."[11]

Bart Campolo has undergone a paradigm shift of his primary beliefs. He no longer sees the world through the lens of the biblical narrative. His loss of faith began when new ideas he had come to accept couldn't be incorporated into his Christian paradigm. His experience should serve as a warning. Losing faith in Jesus is a real possibility for those who—for whatever reason—find themselves in the process of deconstruction. It happened to Bart, and it could have happened to either of us. It can happen to you.[12] For now, keep this in mind: many, if not most, serious Christians go through a process of evaluating what they believe without losing their faith, but that doesn't mean the danger isn't real.

Danger 2: Heresy

Marcion of Sinope was pronounced a heretic and excommunicated by the church in AD 144. What is a heretic? Why was Marcion labeled a heretic? Why should you care? Good questions. The word *heresy* comes from the Geek word *hairesis*, meaning "to choose." A heretic is one who chooses to follow his or her own views even though they conflict with those established by authorities. For our purposes, a heretic is someone who denies the central, orthodox beliefs of the Christian church. When considered in this light, Marcion certainly deserves the label heretic.

Marcion's views about God were radically different from what early Christians had always believed. He taught that there were two Gods. Yahweh, the God of the Old Testament, was a wrathful, violent deity who wanted to keep humanity under his thumb.[13] Abba, the kind God of the New Testament, sent Jesus to save us from Yahweh's wrath. Because of Yahweh's association with the Old Testament, Marcion rejected it as sacred Scripture. He even created his own canon, or list of sacred books. It included only his edited version of the gospel of Luke and ten of Paul's letters! Marcion also denied that Jesus was truly human, a view known as Docetism.

Given his grievous errors, the church had to call him out as a heretic. His teaching was so far from what Christians believed about God, the Bible, and Jesus that he couldn't be considered a Christian any more than someone could be considered a Muslim who rejects Muhammad as a prophet and the Qur'an as inspired scripture.

The church has always understood that it's a fine line between exploring who God is and distorting the Bible's concept of God. As theologian Justin Holcomb points out, "Most of those dubbed heretics were usually asking legitimate and important questions. They weren't heretics because they asked the questions. It is the answers that they gave that are wrong. They went too far by trying to make the Christian faith more compatible with ideas that they already found appealing, especially those of pagan Greek philosophy."[14]

By "too far" Holcomb means the answers the heretics offered led them to tread on dangerous theological ground that, on biblical grounds, placed their salvation in jeopardy. It's not that the early Christians were a bunch of theological sticklers who thought salvation was a matter of passing a doctrine test. They knew that having a relationship with God was a matter of the heart as much as the head. But they were convinced that before the heart can be rightly aligned with God, the head must know who God is. And that required having correct beliefs about him according to the Bible.

This is why the New Testament is filled with warnings about the danger of false teachers. Consider only a few of them:

> Beware of false prophets, who come to you in sheep's clothing but inwardly are ravenous wolves. (Matt. 7:15)

> See to it that no one takes you captive through hollow and deceptive philosophy, which depends on human tradition and the elemental spiritual forces of this world rather than on Christ. (Col. 2:8 NIV)

> Therefore, dear friends, since you have been forewarned, be on your guard so that you may not be carried away by the error of the lawless and fall from your secure position. (2 Peter 3:17 NIV)

> Anyone who runs ahead and does not continue in the teaching of Christ does not have God; whoever continues in the teaching has both the Father and the Son. (2 John 1:9 NIV)

Notice that last verse. Serious error, defined as that which is outside "the teaching of Christ," results in a person not having a relationship with God. It's important to note, however, that the early church didn't think every incorrect belief was heretical. Just those that contradicted the essential elements of the faith, not disagreements on nonessential doctrines.[15]

What does all this talk of heresy have to do with deconstruction? Quite a lot. Deconstruction usually begins with questioning a Christian belief or practice you've always taken for granted. There is nothing inherently wrong with this. Nor is there anything wrong with changing your mind about various practices and beliefs. Rather, it can be good! But it can also be dangerous. The danger is that as you let go of some old beliefs and adopt new ones, at some point your faith may no longer reflect historic Christianity; that is, you may no longer adhere to the teachings of Jesus Christ revealed in Scripture. False teachers still exist and lead people astray. Sincere but wrongheaded teachers also lead people astray. It may sound harsh, but remember, Jesus considered such false prophets to be "wolves in sheep's clothing."

As Holcomb said, heretics often transgress by trying to make the Christian faith more compatible with ideas they find appealing. They also transgress by trying to distance the Christian faith from ideas they find offensive and embarrassing. What people find offensive and embarrassing changes from generation to generation. Today, some of those key issues are the Bible's teaching on marriage as the one-flesh union of one man and one woman, the wrath of God, the sinfulness of humanity, and the exclusivity of Christ as the only means of salvation. What is crucial to understand is that at some point (determining that exact point can be difficult), redefining, rejecting, and reinterpreting enough primary biblical truths results not in a watered-down version of Christianity but a different faith altogether.

Demolition

Several years ago, I (John) returned to my hometown and drove past the old motel where I used to work. I couldn't believe my eyes. There was still a motel there, but not the one I worked at.

A new motel had taken its place. The new one, however, wasn't the result of renovating each room until the entire motel was "new." No, the old motel had been demolished, and a new one built on a different foundation. The new one looked nothing like the original. If the motel were a paradigm, we would say it had undergone a complete shift. The old was gone, and an entirely new one had taken its place.

Whether a person has a paradigm shift that causes them to renounce their faith, like Bart Campolo, or they adopt false teaching and become a heretic, their faith has undergone a paradigm shift. In the case of folks like Bart who deconvert, it's clear that if they once had a relationship with God, they no longer do. Heretics may still identify as Christians, but if their beliefs differ enough from historic Christianity as revealed in Scripture, they can no longer *meaningfully* be called Christians, even if they insist on being called such. At some point, their false beliefs preclude them from having a relationship with God. They are those who, using the New Testament's language, are "without God" because they did not continue in the teachings of Christ. Such is the danger of deconstruction.

Apostasy and heresy are two ways you can fall off the paddleboard as you seek to return to shore. Nevertheless, we're convinced that deconstruction doesn't have to result in a paradigm shift. God has provided us resources to help us keep "the faith which was once delivered unto the saints" (Jude 1:3 KJV). One of those is the church. If you're willing to accept the boundary conditions the church has provided throughout the centuries, you can both deconstruct what you believe and retain a robust, Christian faith. In chapter 4 we'll look at what those boundary conditions are. But first we need to establish the required foundation of any faith that is worthy of the name "Christian."

1. How did you feel as you read Bart Campolo's story? What lessons about deconstruction might you draw from it?

2. Mark Karris traced the seeds of his deconstruction to an event at church that shook him to his core and made him ask hard questions about his faith. Have you had a similar experience?

3. What benefits do you believe can come from rethinking faith?

4. Think about your paradigm, the glasses you see the world through. Would you say it is flexible and able to incorporate new and maybe challenging ideas, or is it inflexible, not admitting ideas that might cause you to reevaluate secondary beliefs? Which—flexible or inflexible—do you think is more susceptible to a faith crisis?

5. How do you respond to the strong statements in the New Testament about the importance of correct doctrine? Why do you think correct belief mattered so much to the New Testament writers?

CHAPTER 3

Who Do You Say That I Am?

*True Christianity is an all-out
commitment to the Lord Jesus Christ.*
—WILLIAM MacDonald

*Why do you call me, "Lord, Lord,"
and do not do what I say?*
—Jesus, Luke 6:46 NIV

Imagine for a moment that you're remodeling a building. Two steps are involved in any remodel. First, you must dismantle certain sections of the building. Second, you have to put them back together again differently than before. There are a lot of ways you can go about dismantling a building, but one thing is certain: if you stand on it while you tear it down, you'll go crashing down with it. To dismantle a building, you need to stand back from it.

Deconstructing one's faith is a lot like remodeling a building. It's an exercise in taking apart and then reassembling a belief system. Both remodeling a building and deconstructing one's faith have a set of tools to accomplish the task. Dismantling a building uses sledgehammers, crowbars, and jackhammers. Deconstructing your faith utilizes the tools of question-asking, reflection, and analysis to question beliefs taken for granted. Remodeling a building requires a solid place to stand; so too does deconstructing your personal faith. In other words, deconstructing your faith requires a foundational theological commitment that's exempt from analysis, which is to say that deconstruction can't even start without a belief that's immune from suspicion. In matters of faith deconstruction, there must be at least one theological given. The question is, What could that theological bedrock be? Is there one foundational, non-negotiable belief of Christianity that can't be questioned, but from which all other beliefs can be? Yes, there is, and his name is Jesus.

What Do You Say?

Christianity isn't first and foremost a set of beliefs. Christianity is first and foremost a person. Jesus is Christianity. That's why the first followers of Jesus were called "Christians" (Acts 11:26). The name *Christianity* literally means "the religion derived from Christ."[1] He's the hinge on which the door of the religion hangs. He's the foundation on which the entire house of faith is built. You can take off the roof, pull off the siding, remove the windows, and even take away the frame, but if you break apart the foundation, there's nothing left to build on.

If you're serious about rethinking your faith and you're equally serious about remaining a Christian, then the deconstruction stops with Jesus. He's the bedrock of Christianity. That's not to say you shouldn't pursue refining your concept of Jesus. You can and you *should*. We never have a perfect understanding of Jesus. As his followers, we ought always to seek a clearer and more accurate picture of him. But Jesus himself established boundaries that the refining process must stay within. Otherwise, you will have moved off the foundation and onto theological quicksand.

The title of this chapter ("Who Do You Say That I Am?") echoes a question Jesus once put to his disciples (Matt. 16:15). Impulsive as usual, Peter spoke up and declared, "You are the Christ, the Son of the living God" (v. 16). Those who follow Jesus recognize that's a good answer even though it requires some explanation and exploration. Getting a handle on what is meant by "Christ" and "Son of the living God" helps establish the foundation on which any authentic version of Christianity must be built. The term *Christ* comes from the Greek word meaning "anointed one" and is related to the Hebrew word translated as *Messiah*. *Christ* is a title, not a last name. It indicates that Jesus is God's anointed representative, sent to be the savior-king of the new kingdom that God is building. The title Son of God indicates that Jesus is literally "of God," which means even though he was human, he shared in God's very nature, making him divine. Now, we doubt Peter understood all the theological implications of his statement at the time, but his answer to Jesus's question indicates that the man Jesus of Nazareth was (and *is*) the Messiah and the divine, sovereign authority over all creation. We believe affirming those two claims is crucial to having a solid foundation on which to rebuild your house of faith.

Jesus wasn't just a rabbi. He wasn't just a prophet. He wasn't just a miracle worker. No, Jesus is the Christ who was prophesied in the Old Testament. As Christ he is Lord, and as Lord he is God. As such, Jesus sets the rules for human beings. He calls the shots, and he says that those who love him will obey him (John 14:15). As you rethink Christianity, it's important to appreciate that, according to Jesus himself, he is the one who determines what it means to be a Christian. Christianity begins and ends with him. Therefore, to deconstruct what you believe without sinking your faith, it's imperative to make sure you have at minimum a correct conception of who he is.

Jesus's discussion with Peter reveals that there are at least two nonnegotiable aspects of Jesus. The first has to do with Jesus's identity as Christ. Having a minimally correct concept of his identity is necessary to be a Christian. Without it, you're not in the kingdom. John says that the one who denies that Jesus is the Christ is a liar who does not have eternal life (1 John 2:22–25). The identity of Jesus is serious business. The second nonnegotiable has to do with how we must respond to him as Lord. Unless our posture toward Jesus is correct, we won't be willing to let him define what it means to be a Christian. We'll take that prerogative for ourselves and, in doing so, create Christianity in our image, not his. Again, the demons correctly understood the identity of Jesus. When Jesus came to their town, the two demon-possessed men identified Jesus as the "Son of God" (Matt. 8:28–29). They had a good theological understanding of Jesus's identity, but they rejected him as Lord. Correct beliefs alone about Jesus are not enough. Jesus's identity as the divine Son of God and our response to him as Lord is the place where the dismantling aspect of deconstruction must end and from which the rebuilding begins.

Cognitive Content: His Identity

Getting Jesus's identity right is crucial in deconstructing faith. It is acceptable for believers to be wrong about a lot of conclusions we come to as we deconstruct and reconstruct our faith. And having wrong ideas has consequences, but none so drastic as having wrong ideas about Jesus. We want to be sure this sinks in, so we will say it in a different way: *your conclusions about the identity of Jesus are the most important thing about you.* That's why Jesus asked his disciples, "Who do you say that I am?" (Mark 8:29).

Imagine you decide to talk with a friend about Jesus and in response she cuts you off and says, "Oh, I know all about that guy. He was an angelic being who masqueraded as a first-century Egyptian shepherd. He saved the world by solving a riddle presented to him by the gods of the underworld. I've committed my life to him." We suspect you'd conclude your friend isn't really a Christian no matter how sincere her belief in "Jesus" is. That's because you recognize that her concept of Jesus doesn't match up with the *real* Jesus. If her concept doesn't match up with the real Jesus, then her faith isn't in the real Jesus. That's a problem because it's only the real Jesus who saves. Since her faith isn't in the real Jesus but in an altogether different "Jesus," she isn't a Christian in any meaningful sense of the word. By the way, we're not uniquely picking on your friend. If we have a faulty view of Jesus, then *we* can't be saved either. This applies to all of us.

Another way of saying this is that it's not the *sincerity* of your faith that saves you, but the *object* you place your faith in. Today we often hear people say, "Live your truth," as if we each have our own truths that we can choose to live out. The reality is that we can have our own *beliefs*, but we can't have our own *truths*. If our beliefs don't match up with reality, then they're not true. Period. We can both sincerely believe we're seven feet tall, but reality says otherwise. It doesn't matter how sincere we are in that belief. Here's a point many people miss today: we can be *sincerely wrong*. The reverse is true as well: we can be *insincerely right*. Sincerity is irrelevant to whether something is true or false. This matters because a sincere belief in Jesus requires an accurate view of his identity.

If we can be saved only by the real Jesus, then isn't it vital we have a correct view of his identity? This is why the character of Jesus and what we believe about him gets a lot of attention in the New Testament. Paul and John were both deeply concerned about the danger of getting Jesus's identity wrong. False teachers, those who did not hold to the teaching of the apostles, had infiltrated the early churches and were leading them astray about the identity of Jesus. Consequently, the apostles picked up their pens and went to battle, writing several letters to groups of Christians about the importance of getting Jesus's identity right. It's not an overstatement to say the apostles saw the issue of Jesus's identity as having central importance and eternal consequences.

Commitment Issues: Our Response

The second essential issue concerning Jesus is his lordship. Besides having an accurate conception of his messianic and divine identity, you also must have a commitment to the lordship of Jesus if you want to remain in the Christian faith. That can't be deconstructed. It's nonnegotiable. By "can't be deconstructed," we don't mean it's not possible to ask questions about Jesus or what he taught. Asking questions about Jesus is good if it's done to pursue truth and with the intent to obey him. We certainly don't mean you have no choice but to believe that Jesus is the Son of God. You are free to reject Jesus as divine, but in doing so, you would no longer be a Christian in any historical or meaningful sense.

Logically speaking, believing in Jesus but not submitting to him as Lord is like believing you have a supervisor at work whose authority you are under but not acting like they're your boss. Not doing what they ask you, ignoring them when they talk, showing up late for work—doing that would get you fired!

Accepting Jesus on our terms isn't orthodox Christianity. We submit to him on *his* terms. His terms are that he's not only savior but also Lord of heaven and earth. The lordship of Jesus has been the cornerstone of Christianity right from the beginning. Throughout history, Christians have disagreed over how to understand some of the things Jesus said and debated how to live them out, but one thing the universal church has always agreed on is that Jesus is Lord. In fact, confessing "Jesus is Lord" was the first creed of the church (Rom. 10:9). Thus, when we say Jesus "can't be deconstructed" as you rethink your faith, we mean that recognizing him as Lord is nonnegotiable for being a genuine Christ follower. It's also the key to discovering the authentic Christianity you're looking for. Unless you're committed to Jesus as Lord, you might be tempted to adopt a view of Jesus that is more fitting to your desires or our cultural moment instead of discovering the true Jesus who came in human flesh two thousand years ago.

Between a Rock and a Hard Place

All right, so let's say you agree with us: a minimally correct understanding of Jesus and the right heart posture toward him are foundational to be a Christian. The next question is, What does that mean? What does it look like to live it out? At the very least, it means wanting to affirm and intending to obey whatever Jesus teaches. That's what it means to say, "Jesus is Lord." At the same time, no one perfectly obeys Jesus's teachings all the time. We certainly don't! Thankfully, it's not our success but our intent that's the issue. Despite all our failures to do so, we should *want* to affirm his teachings and *intend* to obey him. That's the key. Hopefully our success in doing that grows as we mature in the faith.

Affirming his teachings and obeying Jesus sounds simple

enough. Until you read what he said. Then it's not. Jesus said many things that are hard to understand, such as not putting new wine into old wineskins. What's up with that? He also said many things that seem offensive and are impossible to follow literally. Once he told his Jewish audience that unless they ate his flesh and drank his blood, they couldn't follow him! Is it any wonder that a bunch of people walked away after that? Many of Jesus's early followers left him because they couldn't or wouldn't accept what he taught. Jesus's command to the rich young ruler—to sell all he had and give it away to the poor and *then* come follow him—was so difficult that he walked away; and Jesus let him go (Mark 10:22).

At one point Jesus asked his disciples if they were going to leave him too. That's the same question we need to wrestle with today. Sadly, many who deconstruct eventually deconvert because they can't accept or will not submit to what Jesus has to say. But leaving the faith is nobler than thinking we can redefine Christianity on our terms. A self-styled discipleship isn't an option Jesus offers us. If he's Lord, then he determines what it means to be a Christian, not us. After all, the religion is named after him.

The Meaning of It All

If the most important question that needs answering is, Who do you say that I am? the second most important question is, How do I determine what Jesus wants? The easy answer is that we read his Word, the Bible. But now the real problem comes into focus. The Bible needs to be interpreted, and at the end of the day we're the ones who determine which interpretations we'll adopt. This challenge is inescapable. When we read the Bible, sometimes we come across things that make us think, "Really, God said *that*?" And we're faced with a choice: Will we accept what the Bible teaches or find a way to avoid it?

One particularly difficult Christian teaching is the doctrine of eternal punishment. The Bible portrays the final state of those who reject Christ as a lake of fire (Rev. 20:13–15). What a terrifying and deeply disturbing thing to read. How can we reconcile a God of love with people being tormented for eternity in a lake of fire? It seems contradictory. The tension we feel when we think about a lake of fire is the result of our moral intuition conflicting with what the Bible appears to teach.

When faced with a seeming incompatibility between the teaching of Scripture and our moral intuition, it's valid to ask if Scripture *means* what it appears to *say*. Maybe there's another way to legitimately understand the text that resolves the tension. Our moral intuition is a gift from God that prompts us when something is wrong. When a passage in the Bible triggers that intuition, it might mean we should take a second look at the passage in question. Maybe we have misunderstood the passage. At the same time, we need to remember that our moral intuition isn't an infallible guide. It would be wrong to adopt an interpretation that fits with our moral intuition if doing so requires interpretive gymnastics to make the Bible say what we want it to say. Sometimes it is our moral intuitions that need refining. Yet is it possible, without twisting the Bible into knots, that we might understand the lake of fire as something other than a divine torture chamber? We think the answer is yes. In fact, we think such teaching is not only more in line with moral intuition but also the best scriptural interpretation given the genre and context of Revelation. But if after a deep dive into studying the matter we concluded that the Bible does teach that the lake of fire is just that, a literal lake of fire, the lordship of Jesus requires we submit to what the Bible teaches. Of course, another option is to abandon Christianity entirely. But if Jesus really is God and he taught that hell is a literal lake of fire, then isn't it reasonable to conclude that his moral understanding is superior to ours and he understands something even when we don't? After all, Jesus sees things with perfect moral clarity and we have imperfect, tainted vision in our present fallen state (1 Cor. 13:12).

Jesus's lordship is a nonnegotiable for followers of Jesus. But our interpretations of what Jesus taught aren't. His teachings are always interpreted through the various lenses we wear. One of those, which we just mentioned, is our moral intuition. Another is a lens that hates to submit to anyone but ourselves, a lens of independence. That should give us pause when we encounter a teaching in the Bible we don't like. Maybe it's our rebellious nature trying to call the shots because it doesn't want to submit to Scripture. Scripture is unmistakable about the corruption of the human heart (Mark 7:20–23; Rom. 3:23; 1 John 1:8). Even though we are new creatures in Christ, we aren't yet fully freed from the effects of sin and must be vigilant not to read Scripture in a way that reflects our personal desires.

How do we know how to read God's Word under the lordship of Jesus while wearing these two lenses that influence our interpretation? There's no perfect method for doing so. The principles of hermeneutics, the art and science of interpretation, are important to follow as we wrestle with Scripture. Admittedly, there are different approaches to hermeneutics, but most agree on the fundamental principles of interpreting texts well. Equally, if not more, important as a good method is having the right attitude as we approach Scripture. Humility, intellectual honesty, and commitment to the truth are crucial. This is partly why Proverbs 9:10 says that wisdom begins with the fear of the Lord. It is only when we understand the character of God and stand humbly before him that we can grow in knowledge and wisdom. Clothing ourselves with those virtues will not guarantee the correct interpretation, but it can help us minimize the effects of our sinfulness and ultimately allow us to stand before the Lord with a clear conscience that we handled his Word well (2 Tim. 2:15).

We'll address the Bible further in chapter 5. For now, it's important to grasp that the cry "Jesus is Lord" implies a desire to obey what he teaches. Jesus is the bedrock of Christianity. It's the place where anyone deconstructing their faith must stand and the foundation on which any reconstruction must be built. Without Jesus, *everything* crumbles.

Bait and Switch?

Nothing we've said so far either presumes or entails any particular vision of what it means to be a Christian. Committing yourself to the lordship of Jesus doesn't mean you'll inevitably end up in the very same version of Christianity you are questioning. Although we both come from a conservative evangelical tradition, the claim that Jesus is the divine Son of God who is Lord over all isn't an evangelical claim. It's a Christian claim. Period. Full stop.

Many visions and flavors of Christianity are compatible with that claim. We are just laying out the broadest boundary marker that limits the length and breadth of the shoreline you hope to return to. Borders separate one nation from another. When you cross over them, you are in another country. The same is true with the basic contours of the Christian faith. There are boundary markers. Cross them and you're not within the Christian faith anymore. The most basic is your view of Jesus and your attitude toward him.

We're less concerned with what you believe about secondary and tertiary issues of the Christian faith than we are about the beliefs in your mind and the posture of your heart toward Jesus. Our goal is to help you figure out *how* you can have a genuine and meaningful commitment to Jesus. That's the heart of Christianity. That's the goal of this book.

In the fog of deconstruction, determining to make Jesus your north star and committing yourself to his lordship are the first steps to making it back to shore. When you do that, the fog will begin to dissipate, allowing you to know in which direction to start paddling.

Reflection Questions

1. Jesus has to be the foundation of any legitimate Christian deconstruction. Thus, seeking a better understanding of Jesus is important. What's the difference between seeking a better understanding of Jesus and deconstructing Jesus as the foundation?

2. What do you think of our claim that each person can have their own belief but not their own truth? Do you agree? What's the difference between belief and truth?

3. If you're a Christian, then Jesus has saved you, and that's good news! But sometimes as Christians we may not have come to terms with what it fully means to recognize Jesus as Lord. Do you think someone who believes in Jesus as savior but does not live like he is Lord will be saved? Why or why not?

4. Does the Bible have any issues that trigger your moral intuition and make you want to find a way to explain the problem away even if it means twisting what the Bible appears to teach?

5. Imagine that you are standing in the center of campus with Jesus and he has given a very unpopular speech on a number of controversial topics. A lot of people are offended and begin plotting how to cancel him. It's even too much for some of Jesus's acquaintances, who abandon him. In the middle of all this, he turns to you and says, "What about you? Will you also leave?" How might you respond?

CHAPTER 4

Fences

Whenever you remove any fence,
always pause long enough to ask why
it was put there in the first place.
—John F. Kennedy

Describing something helps to define
it, to give it limits, to set guardrails
of understanding around it.
—Jim Butcher

As a society, we've become increasingly sensitive about the ethical treatment of animals. This is especially true when it comes to the farming industry. More than ever, we care how animals, including those that eventually become our food, are treated. It's hard not to be troubled at the sight of chickens crammed into enclosures twenty-four hours a day without sunlight or cows in feed lots, packed into pens by the thousands to fatten them up. You don't have to be an animal rights activist to wish there was a way to get an omelet or hamburger without such restrictive and harsh conditions for the animals.

Because of increased attention brought by folks deeply concerned about the welfare of animals such as chickens, cows, and pigs, an alternative method of raising livestock has become popular. This method, known as free-range farming, allows animals to live outdoors in their natural environment. Free to roam, the animals benefit from both the natural sunlight and the exercise. They also don't suffer from the stress of overcrowded enclosures. But the label "free-range" is a bit misleading. While the animals are allowed to wander around and investigate large swaths of land, their ability to do so is restricted. At some point they bump up against a fence. Free-range farmers are willing to give their animals some freedom to move about the pasture, but to keep them from leaving the farm, they put up fences. Otherwise, the animals would wander off and likely be attacked by a predator. Though free range farmers do believe enclosures can be harmful, they see the necessity of fences. So did the early Christians.

Since the beginning of the church, there's been a need for "fences" that keep Christians from wandering off the theological "farm." Unfortunately, the need for theological fences, which are good and necessary, has been abused. Some Christian traditions don't allow for diverse thought within appropriate boundaries. Some use theological fences to control rather than protect. Some stifle legitimate freedom by requiring uniformity of thought and practice on *all* issues. In doing so, they shrink the large pasture of historic Christianity to a restrictive and cramped enclosure.

If one of the reasons you're deconstructing is because you feel like you're trapped in a Christian tradition that acts more like an enclosure than a pasture, take heart. We understand and are sorry you've had such a constricting experience with faith. It's not meant to be that way! In this chapter, we want to give you the liberty to be a *free-range believer*. By free-range believer, we mean a follower of Jesus who has permission to roam the pasture of Christian doctrine and think, analyze, and adopt a wide variety of beliefs within Christian orthodoxy. There's no reason you need to choose between either living in the restrictive enclosure of your present tradition or leaving the faith. There's middle ground to be had. Free-range believers have choice within broad limits. Make no mistake, there *are* limits. Without them Christians would, like chickens, wander off and become susceptible to theological predators.

Relative Importance

Frank lives across the street from my (John's) house, in his car. He's a great guy, but for years he's struggled with addiction that's taken a toll on his life. We don't know each other well, but occasionally Frank and I have the opportunity to chat. One day our conversation turned to spiritual things, and Frank took the opportunity to share with me what he excitedly called "the most important news ever." That's right, Frank explained the gospel to me. I kept trying to interrupt him to let him know I was a believer too, but to no avail. He kept right on going, telling me how I could have a relationship with God. "Frank," I finally got the chance to say, "I'm a Christian too. I believe the gospel."

"That's great," he said. "Now let me tell you about the second most important news ever!"

"What's that?" I inquired. That's when Frank laid on me the second most important news. He paused, looked me in the eye, and whispered, "The cold medicine Zicam cures COVID, but nobody knows it!"

I'm convinced that Frank is wrong about Zicam curing

COVID. But, bless his heart, he's right: *not all news is of equal importance*. Even if Zicam did cure COVID, it's still not the most important news. The news about how we can have a relationship with God is of greater importance than curing the coronavirus. What's true about what Frank called "important news" is also true about Christian beliefs. They're not all equal in importance.

Saying that not all beliefs having to do with Christianity are equal in importance shouldn't be controversial. The truth that the biblical judge Ehud was left-handed isn't nearly as important as the theme of the book of Judges, which is that sin has devastating consequences when people do what is right in their own eyes (Judg. 17:6). The question is, How do we determine which beliefs are the most important? A series of concentric circles is a helpful model some theologians propose. The circle at the center of the model contains the beliefs that need to be affirmed to be rightly related to Jesus and to be considered a Christian, theologically speaking. These are known as "dogma." Examples of some dogmatic beliefs are the triune character of God; the humanity, deity, and resurrection of Jesus; and that salvation is by faith alone in Christ's work on the cross. More could be added. But it's important to point out that to be in God's family, you don't necessarily have to *affirm* every dogma. Salvation isn't a matter of passing a theology exam. But there are some beliefs that you can't *deny* and still be rightly related to Jesus or called a Christian, theologically speaking.[1] As we'll see, these beliefs establish the boundaries of how far the word *Christian* can be stretched. To deny dogma and still call yourself a Christian is a contradiction in terms.

The next circle contains those beliefs known as "doctrine." Doctrines are beliefs derived from dogma. An example of doctrine is a belief someone might hold about the timing of the second coming of Jesus. All Christians believe Jesus is going to return. That's dogma. But not everyone agrees *when* that event will happen. Doctrinal beliefs are important, but not as important as dogma. Individuals and groups can disagree over doctrines and still be within the bounds of historic Christianity. Disagreements over doctrine are usually the result of interpretive differences. Many doctrinal differences exist within the church. In fact, you can trace the origins of most denominations to differences over doctrine.

The third circle, the one furthest from the center, comprises different ways of interpreting doctrines. Beliefs in this circle might be considered as opinions. You might believe that the millennial reign of Jesus will be an earthly geopolitical kingdom, but your friend thinks it will be a spiritual kingdom where Jesus reigns in the hearts of his followers. This is an interesting biblical question to explore, but it is not tied to salvation, and churches should not divide over it.

In this chapter we're going to focus on the two inner circles, but we're going to use the metaphor of a pasture in which the outer fence represents dogma and the inner pasture represents doctrine. As you rethink what it means to follow Jesus, the beliefs in these two areas are what matter most.

Dogma: A Needed Fence

From the time of the first Christians to the current day, followers of Jesus have recognized a core set of claims that establish the boundaries of the faith. The earliest expression of that core was called the "rule of faith." The rule of faith was the first rudimentary fence placed around the pasture of Christian belief. The rule of faith took various forms, but it always proclaimed certain truths: there's one God; God became man in Jesus Christ; Jesus died, rose again, and will come again. These beliefs were universally acknowledged in the church as the essential boundaries of the faith established by the apostles. In the years after the apostles' deaths, early leaders in the church, such as Irenaeus and Tertullian, appealed to the rule of faith in refuting those who promoted heretical teachings.[2] It served as the earliest fence to keep God's people within genuine Christianity.

Over time, more destructive teachings cropped up within young churches. Even though the early church allowed for a diversity of beliefs, some groups were promoting beliefs that went beyond the limits of biblically acceptable diversity. The rule of faith needed to be expanded to address these false teachings. In time, the church crafted more comprehensive statements identifying what individuals needed to affirm to be considered Christian. We call those statements "creeds," and they pinpoint essential Christian beliefs, what we're calling dogma.

Creeds are a summary of the teachings of the New Testament and a window into how the early church formulated the heart of the Christian faith.[3] Theologian Michael Bird maintains that "the creeds drew a line between faith derived from Scripture and understood in light of apostolic testimony and a different kind of faith emerging from pagan philosophy and incoherent readings of Scripture" and that the "creeds are the gold standard by which one can safeguard the fixtures of our faith that are of first importance and warn against falsehood by those who would dangerously fiddle with the crucial facets of the faith."[4]

The church has crafted several creeds throughout its history. But three of the earliest and most important are the Apostles' Creed (AD 200), the Nicene Creed (AD 325), and the Athanasian Creed (fifth century AD).[5] These three are known as the ecumenical creeds because they proclaim the beliefs that the church has widely affirmed.

Ultimately, the Bible, not the creeds, is the standard for

orthodox belief. However, while the majority of the New Testament books were utilized in the church and understood as canonical much earlier, the New Testament canon as we know it today wasn't solidified until the fourth century. In the meantime, with heretical teaching appearing inside and outside the church, believers needed to know which beliefs were authentically Christian, and the creeds clarified these essential Christian beliefs.

Today, Christians have the New Testament, but the creeds are still of great importance. They help us read the New Testament faithfully by providing us with a window into what early Christians understood to be an accurate summary of the New Testament's core teachings. Thus, if a present-day teacher offers an interpretation of Scripture that violates the creeds, we ought to reject it. In short, because they are rooted in Scripture, the creeds act as the fences that mark the boundaries between Christian and non-Christian beliefs.

What Good Are Fences?

But are fences necessary? Can't we just pick and choose what to believe about Christianity? Isn't questioning the creeds what deconstruction is all about? Not quite. As you deconstruct, the fences that the creeds establish aren't only important but also necessary. Without them, it's unlikely that you'll remain a Christian. The creedal fences perform two vital services: they *protect* us from theological danger and *define* what biblical Christianity actually is. Both are crucial to understanding and having a faithful deconstruction.

1. FENCES SAVE LIVES

In December 2015, actor James Woods was traveling along the I-70 freeway just outside Glenwood Springs, Colorado, when disaster struck. Another car traveling in the same direction at seventy-five miles per hour hit an ice patch and spun out. Woods quickly swerved into the wall of the mountain to avoid the spinning vehicle. Fortunately, he avoided the car, but he bounced off the wall, spun 180 degrees, and careened out of control. Woods was sliding backward at sixty miles per hour toward the other side of the road and the one-hundred-foot drop to the river below. The only thing between him and flying off the cliff to his death was the guardrail. Thankfully for Woods, it did its job and stopped his Jeep 4×4 before it plunged over the cliff. He walked away without serious injury.

James Woods's harrowing tale is just one of thousands of similar stories where a guardrail kept a driver from death or serious injury. Guardrails are a kind of fence, and anyone who's driven on a road notched out of the side of a mountain knows their importance. Without them, the drive would be not only terrifying but also life threatening. Treacherous mountain roads aren't the only place where having guardrails is important.

As we read the New Testament, some of the things that repeatedly jump off its pages are the warnings written to the early Christians that they were in danger of driving headlong off several theological cliffs. That is, they were in danger of believing things that put their faith and salvation in jeopardy.

To ensure that early believers held correct spiritual views, the apostles constructed theological guardrails to keep believers from veering off the road into heresy. Indeed, many of the New Testament books are written specifically for that purpose! As you rethink what it means to be a Christian, we urge you to respect the guardrail of the three ecumenical creeds. If you don't, your deconstruction will look a lot like James Woods heading toward the cliff, but in your case, there'll be nothing to keep you from going over it.

2. FENCES DETERMINE MEANING

In the book *Through the Looking-Glass* (the sequel to *Alice's Adventures in Wonderland*), Alice has a frustrating conversation with Humpty Dumpty. What makes the conversation so maddening is that Humpty Dumpty rejects the accepted definitions of words. Instead, he invents his own definitions. Words mean what he decides they mean. "'When I use a word,' Humpty Dumpty said in a rather scornful tone, 'it means just what I choose it to mean—neither more nor less.'"[6] Alice wisely suspected Humpty Dumpty's ability to make words mean what he wants them to. "'The question is,' said Alice, 'whether you can make words mean so many different things.'"[7]

What Alice understood was that if words can mean different things to different people, then they mean nothing to everyone else. Another way of saying it is that a word's meaning needs limitations, or fences, if it's to have any meaning at all.

Words are symbols that stand for something else. Whatever they stand for, that thing sets the limits of the meaning of the word. For example, the English-speaking community has chosen the letters D-O-G as the sign that represents a certain kind of animal with specific traits. Another set of letters could have been chosen to refer to that animal. In French the word is *chien*, in Spanish it's *perro*. What each of these symbols stands for is a kind of animal. Not every animal, but one specific kind of animal. What makes a particular animal (Fido) a member of that kind are its essential traits. The essential traits of the animal set the limits as to what can legitimately be called a dog. The essential traits of a *dog* are "a domesticated carnivorous mammal that typically has a long snout, an acute sense of smell, nonretractable claws, and a barking, howling, or whining voice."[8]

When a child says "doggie" and points to an animal that adults call a cat, the adult corrects the child and says, "No, no. That's a cat." The English word *cat*, or in French *chat*,

Spanish *gato*, picks out a particular kind of animal with different essential characteristics. Whether dog or cat, the essential characteristics of a particular animal make it the kind of thing it is. Humans recognize things and give them names. The name is limited to those things, and only those things that have those essential characteristics.[9]

Like the words *dog* or *cat*, the word *Christian* stands for something specific. It refers to the core of apostolic and postapostolic teachings expressed in the creeds that form the common consensus of the faith and define what it means to be Christian.[10] Those are the "essential characteristics" of what the word *Christian* refers to. A person can call their unique set of beliefs "Christian" all they want, but if it differs from the core of the apostolic and postapostolic teaching, doing so will not make it Christian any more than calling a cat a "dog" will make it bark. If we say that each Christian can create their own recipe of beliefs and expect other Christians to acknowledge them as Christian regardless of their conformity to historic Christianity, we risk emptying the term *Christian* of any meaning.[11] Like Humpty Dumpty, people may have the ability to choose their own definitions for words, but they don't have the right to redefine reality.

Fences Require Builders

If fences are necessary for words to have meaning, it raises the question of who gets to build them? As it relates to deconstruction, the question is, Who gets to determine what the word *Christian* means? The answer is those who started the whole thing. Who gets to determine what Tesla or SpaceX is? Elon Musk, because he started the companies. As the creator, he's the only person who has the authority to determine what Tesla is.

Similarly, Jesus and his apostles determine what it means to be a Christian. Jesus chose apostles, in part, so that the Holy Spirit would teach them important truths to pass on when he was gone (John 14:26). The apostles were divinely commissioned. They heard all Jesus's teachings from the beginning and faithfully passed on his teachings. The apostles, and those who knew the apostles or were disciples of those who knew the apostles, get to establish where the fences should be placed. Only they were in the position to know what being a genuine Christian meant. They have passed on that knowledge to us in the New Testament, which has been codified in the form of the creeds. Not recognizing the authority of the apostles to set the boundaries of Christianity and instead setting up your own fence places you outside apostolic and historic Christianity.

Saying we need to stay within the dogmatic boundaries of historic Christianity doesn't mean you have to give up your unique experience of following Jesus. It certainly doesn't mean you have to stop thinking or asking questions. Nor does it mean you must blindly accept every teaching or practice your Christian tradition holds. As mentioned, some Christian traditions require believers to affirm secondary beliefs and practices that restrict freedom to roam. Just remember, not every belief is nonnegotiable. Dogma—the content of the ecumenical creeds—is nonnegotiable for Christ followers. But the creeds leave a lot of theological room within the pasture of doctrine. In *that* circle, there is a tremendous amount of space to roam around theologically without fear of crashing through the fence of dogma.

Doctrine: An Expansive Pasture

Along the north shore of Lake Huron sits the town of Thessalon, Ontario. A small cattle farm in Thessalon stops traffic every year on Canada's main highway in both directions. The blockade isn't a protest or a parade. It's a migration of sorts. Years ago, the Trans-Canada Highway was rerouted. The new portion of the highway goes right through the farm, cutting the barn off from the pasture. In the spring, for the cattle to get from the barn to the pasture, they need to cross the highway. And for all the cows to cross the highway, traffic must stop. On the agreed-upon day, the police bring Canada's national highway to a standstill in both directions, and the cattle begin moving. Once the cattle are across the highway, they find themselves in a large, lush pasture where they can freely roam. Yet, of course, the pasture is surrounded by a fence. Why? Otherwise, the cattle would wander out onto the highway!

If dogma is the fence, then doctrine is the pasture. Like the cattle in Thessalon, Christians are fenced in by the essentials described in the creeds. But within those limits, they're free to explore the expansive "pasture" of Christian doctrine.

Simply put, "doctrine" means teaching, and it's usually used in the context of a specific group. In the case of the Christian faith, doctrine is a body of teaching that a group of Christians hold in reference to their faith. Doctrine varies from group to group for various reasons. But it typically comes down to matters of interpretation. Why do interpretations vary? One reason is because Christians read the Bible with different assumptions that may come from their backgrounds, experiences, or church traditions. While all Christians share common dogma about Jesus, they may have varying doctrines about how to understand his character and how to live out their faith. For example, the creeds teach that God is the creator of heaven and earth. All Christians affirm that, but not all agree on how or when he did it or how long it took. Bible-believing Christians have a range of opinions about how to interpret the first eleven chapters in Genesis. Yet, again, all Christians believe God is the creator and that Scripture is authoritative. Another core Christian teaching is that Jesus is coming back and will judge the world. But when that will happen, how many judgments there will be, where it will take place, and a host of other questions about the end times are open for debate and difference of opinion. Is there a future millennium? Is hell a literal lake of fire, or is that description metaphorical? Will there be an opportunity to repent and be delivered from hell? These and a lot of other questions are legitimate to ask. Christians can, in light of how they understand the Bible, disagree on the doctrines listed previously and many more.

In her book *A Flexible Faith*, Bonnie Kristian focused on seventeen doctrines and, for each, identified the different positions Christians have held regarding them over the last two thousand years. Almost every position she presented was squarely within the bounds of the fence of Christian dogma.[12] What she found shocked her and was reflected in her original title for the book. Are you ready for it? The original title was *200 Million Ways to Follow Jesus* because that's an approximation of how many combinations of belief a Christian could select and still be within the fence of orthodoxy! She said, "Remember the sheer size of that number. It gives a little glimpse of how following Jesus is a big, weird, amazing thing that individual believers, movements, and denominations have expressed in remarkably different ways over the centuries."[13]

Two hundred million ways to be a Christian! Is that free-range enough for you?

Being a Free-Range Believer

The name Francesco Schettino isn't exactly a household name these days. But if you were paying attention to the news in January 2012, he was making headlines for all the wrong reasons. Schettino was a ship captain who wasn't satisfied with freedom within the limits he was afforded by the channel markers of his route on January 13, 2012. That fateful day, Schettino was at the helm of the Italian cruise ship the *Costa Concordia* when he decided to sail it outside the navigational buoys to get a better look at Isola del Giglio, an Italian island in the Tyrrhenian Sea. Instead of keeping the *Concordia* inside the channel markers, he sailed within one thousand feet of the shore. The ship slammed into a rock, took on water, and eventually sank. Tragically, thirty-four people lost their lives in the disaster. The recovery and salvage effort ended up costing over $2 billion. For his role in the accident, Schettino was sentenced to sixteen years in prison.

That accident didn't have to happen. All the heartache and financial ruin could have been avoided if Schettino would have been satisfied with being a free-range captain and sailed the *Costa Concordia* within the established boundaries for the cruise ship. He had plenty of room to maneuver within the given boundaries. Channel markers allowed for a lot of flexibility and freedom to sail the ship. Sadly, leaving the safety of the channel markers didn't even allow for a better view. Still, he chose not to stay within the navigational boundary markers, and it cost him and his passengers greatly.

Captain Schettino and his handling of the *Costa Concordia* is a cautionary tale. The lesson is that we ought to respect established boundary markers. They're there for a reason. We need theological boundaries in the same way that ships need navigational boundary markers—to keep us from shipwrecking our faith. The creeds are those boundary markers. They identify the borders that define the Christian shoreline. It's to a community within these boundaries we encourage you to paddle as you think about the best way to faithfully follow Jesus.[14]

Reflection Questions

1. Are you surprised to hear us say that not all doctrines are of equal importance? Do you agree or disagree with that claim?

2. What beliefs do you think are necessary to be rightly related to God? In other words, what must a person affirm to be saved?

3. Are there any beliefs that do not need to be affirmed to be saved, but that can't be denied? For example, you don't need to affirm the virgin birth of Jesus to be saved. But if you deny it, can you be saved?

4. Have you changed your mind about any doctrines that were handed down to you by your Christian community? If so, what are they and why did you change your mind?

5. Some people suggest that dogma provides fences to set us free? Do you agree, or do you think dogma limits our freedom?

CHAPTER 5

Says Who?

We were given the Scriptures to humble us into realizing that God is right, and the rest of us are just guessing.

—RICH MULLINS

Everything in Scripture has the force of law. What it teaches we are to believe; what it commands, we are to do. We should take its wisdom to heart, imitate its heroes, laugh at its jokes, trust its promises, and sing its songs.

—JOHN FRAME

AirAsia flight D7223 took off on March 10, 2015, from Sydney, Australia, headed for Kuala Lumpur, Malaysia. It eventually arrived after a long and unnecessary delay. Why the delay? The plane began flying *away* from its Malaysian destination. By the time the pilot realized what was happening, it was too late. Unable to fix the problem, he was forced to land in Melbourne, Australia, where the plane sat for hours.

You are probably wondering the same thing as the passengers: what caused the plane to fly so far off course? The explanation was simple. The plane was using the wrong coordinates. Prior to the flight, the pilot manually entered coordinates into the onboard flight navigation system. Instead of entering the plane's longitude correctly as 15109.8 east, he entered it as 01519.8 east. That seemingly small error of misplacing the zero had *massive* consequences. The navigational system would have taken the plane just outside Cape Town, South Africa, some 5,958 miles off course. Instead of flying northwest, the plane flew northeast out over the Pacific Ocean. Had the crew not discovered the error in time, flight D7223 would have ended in disaster.

Before you begin a journey, it's important to enter the right coordinates. Otherwise, your trip might be in trouble *from the start*. This is true for flying planes and for deconstructing one's faith. The difference is that deconstruction isn't guided by geographical coordinates but by theological "coordinates"—that is, assumptions. If you want to have a faithful deconstruction, one that lands you in an authentic expression of Christianity, then having right assumptions at the outset of your journey is vital. For deconstruction, no assumptions are more important than the ones you have about the Bible. What you assume about the Bible will direct and likely determine the course of your journey. Without wanting to be too dramatic, let us state the issue as clearly as we can: your beliefs about the Bible can make the difference between a deconstruction that lands you safely in a community on the Christian shoreline or a paradigm shift that sends you flying out over the ocean in the opposite direction.

Authority Problems

In the movie *U-571*, a damaged German submarine is captured and taken control of by the US Navy. As they attempt to navigate to the safety of a British harbor, they encounter a German plane that is unaware the U-boat has been commandeered by the Americans. The plane circles the sub several times as Lieutenant Andrew Tyler and three of his sailors observe from the deck of the surfaced submarine. Not wanting to give the plane any indication that the U-boat has been taken over by the Americans, Lieutenant Tyler orders Seaman Ronald Parker, who is manning the flak gun, not to shoot at the plane. Then suddenly the plane changes course and instead of circling the submarine it takes an attack posture, flying low and straight at it. Convinced that the plane is about to attack them, the sailors demand that Parker shoot the plane. Lieutenant Tyler, however, commands Seaman Parker to hold his fire. As the plane bears down on the ship, the conflicting commands increase in volume and intensity. It looks for all intents and purposes that the pilot somehow knows they aren't German sailors and is going to blow them out of the water. Nevertheless, Lieutenant Tyler still orders Parker to hold his fire.

What should Seaman Parker do? He has seconds to decide which order he'll submit to: that of his fellow seamen, who are convinced he must shoot down the plane to spare their lives, or the lieutenant, who believes the pilot still assumes they're Germans. In that terrifying moment, Seaman Parker has to determine who his authority is.

When it comes to the Christian life, we're faced with a similar dilemma: Who is our authority in matters of faith and practice? As Christians, we all agree that we should submit to Jesus as our ultimate authority. The question then becomes, Where do we find Jesus's instructions? There are basically two options available. These options are quite different from each other, and as you rethink your faith, you need to decide which you will choose. The option you choose will determine what kind of Christianity you ultimately adopt.

Two Options: Which Will You Choose?

The first option is to view the Bible as a revelation from God that is entirely trustworthy concerning everything it affirms and thus is the guide for what to believe and how to live. On this view, the Bible is true and reliable, and our job is to understand its teachings and then try to live them out faithfully. Simply put, the Bible is authoritative for belief and practice. We'll call this the *historic view* because it has been the dominant position of the church throughout its existence.

The second option is to evaluate the Bible's teachings to determine which parts are trustworthy and reliable. On this view, not everything the Bible affirms accurately reflects God's character or his commands. We discern the parts of Scripture that are trustworthy, and then we determine how to live out those teachings. Because this view assumes Scripture is not entirely trustworthy, it requires one to shift the authority from Scripture to an authority believed to be more trustworthy, such as experience, intuition, culture, or something else. We'll call this the *progressive view* because it looks to an authority outside of and beyond Scripture itself as the final authority.

These two views lie at opposite ends of the spectrum from each other and are irreconcilable. Christians have put forward other more nuanced views as middle positions, but no matter how nuanced a view is, the dividing issue is how it answers the authority question.[1] Does it assign the final authority for faith and practice to the Bible itself, or does it look to something else? Let's take a closer look at the two authority options and see how they differ.

OPTION #1: THE HISTORIC VIEW

When it comes to the authority of the Bible, there is a clear and undeniable historical view held by Christians from the early church fathers all the way up to the present day. The historic view argues that Scripture, from Genesis to Revelation, is inspired by God and trustworthy in what it affirms. To accomplish his purposes, God used individuals to compose, edit, and shape the texts into their final form to accurately communicate his message. Because of the human element involved, the books of the Bible reflect the culture, worldview, and basic assumptions of the people who wrote them. Nevertheless, even though fallible, culturally conditioned humans penned the books of the Bible, God carried their work along through the power of the Holy Spirit to ensure the finished product was entirely trustworthy (see 2 Peter 1:21). Since "all Scripture is breathed out by God and profitable for teaching, for reproof, for correction, and for training in righteousness" (2 Tim. 3:16), it follows that it is the church's final authority on matters of faith and practice.[2] On this view, the written words of Scripture are nothing less than the very words of God himself.

On the historic view, the Bible acts for Christians very much like the Constitution does for judges in the United States. Judges submit to the Constitution as their final authority in matters of law. Judges do their best to interpret what the Constitution says and then apply it to specific cases. Judges approach the Constitution with varied judicial philosophies, but all their decisions are to be grounded in the Constitution. They can't just ignore an amendment they don't like, write it off as outdated, or decide it isn't reflective of America. Judges are under the authority of the Constitution. Unlike the Constitution, though, the Bible is not a collection of laws, but rather a collection of books of various genres that tell the story of God and his people. And yet the parallels for how it should operate within the church are similar. Christians should look to the Bible as their final authority for faith and practice. At the same time, just because the Bible is authoritative for all Christians doesn't mean all Christians understand it the same way.

The Bible, like all communication, needs to be interpreted. Christians can, and definitely do, disagree on what the Bible teaches. This has been the case since the earliest days of the church. In principle, there's no problem with this as long as differing interpretations are characterized by two things. First, they are within the bounds of orthodoxy spelled out earlier. Interpreting the Bible in ways that transgress the dogmas of the faith puts one outside historic Christianity. Second, that we do our best to read *from* what the Bible really teaches rather than read *into* what we want it to teach. Nothing is simpler than finding a way to make the Bible say what we want it to say. But the lordship of Jesus requires that we rigorously resist that temptation. The best antidote to avoiding the temptation to align Scripture with our desires is to purpose in our hearts before the Lord that we will aim to understand it first on its own terms. We do that by evaluating differing interpretations as neutrally as possible.[3] This means weighing the evidence for and against our preferred position as objectively as we can. It also means listening to arguments from all sides and then accepting the one we think does the best job of reflecting the meaning of the text.[4]

OPTION #2: THE PROGRESSIVE VIEW

On my (Sean's) YouTube channel, I interview guests on a variety of topics related to Christianity. Sometimes the guests are fellow believers, sometimes they are committed unbelievers, and sometimes they are somewhere in between. Not long ago, I had a discussion with a pastor who identifies as a "progressive Christian." Although we both call ourselves Christians, we differ significantly on theological and moral issues.

Progressive Christianity is a movement that is difficult to define. That's because many individuals with various perspectives claim the label "progressive." On one hand, some who identify as progressive Christians hold to what has long been known as liberal theology. Liberal theology is a distinct approach to understanding Christianity that denies the uniqueness of Christ as the means of salvation, rejects the miraculous—including the virgin birth and the resurrection of Jesus—and rejects the Bible as the final authority for faith and practice.[5] On the other hand, many who identify as progressive Christians would reject liberal theology almost entirely. These are folks who are orthodox in their basic beliefs about Jesus but who question aspects of fundamentalist or evangelical Christianity. Specifically, they ask about what ought to be the relationship between Christianity and science, the nature of the atonement, the basis of God's judgment, the purpose and duration of condemnation in the afterlife, whether God saves people apart from a cognitive awareness of Jesus, whether there is truth in other religions, and if traditional views of sexual ethics as they relate to LGBTQ need to be reevaluated. All of which is to say, the label "progressive Christianity" can mean a lot of different things to a lot of different people.

But even though there is great diversity among those who identify as progressives, one thing that many, if not most, progressive Christians share or are motivated by is a certain understanding of and approach to the Bible. This was clear in my interview with the progressive Christian pastor. The reason we disagreed on the matter of sexual ethics is because we disagree on how we understand the Bible. Our different positions on homosexuality are not the result of differing interpretations of the Bible. They are the result of different views of the nature and role of the Bible in the Christian life. After our YouTube conversation, he wrote this on his Facebook page:

Last week I participated in an online conversation with a well-known evangelical apologist about our differing opinions on LGBTQ relationships. During the show I asked him, "What would it take for you to change your mind on this?" His response was that he needs better Biblical arguments.

Really?

Think about that. . . . Because of a couple words and ideas, written down by desert dwelling "barely not cave-people anymore" humans, in a massively patriarchal society with zero insight into human psychology and sexuality (at least, in comparison to today) . . . just a handful of thousands year old words have LOCKED people in to a way of thinking where they CANNOT SEE the full humanity of queer people.

What a tragic shame.

Put your damn Bible down for a second and listen to the stories of those who've been told their whole life by the church that they are an abomination.[6]

I appreciate his desire for the church to listen to the voices of LGBTQ individuals so we can love them better. Sadly, as a church, we haven't always done this well. We can—and must—do better. Yet the challenge to "put your damn Bible down and listen to the stories of those who've been told their whole life by the church that they are an abomination" isn't just a call to be more empathetic or compassionate. Rather, it's an appeal to adopt an understanding of the Bible that is significantly different from the historic view we've presented.[7] It's also a view you're likely to encounter and possibly consider as you deconstruct.

According to many progressive Christians, the Bible is not the fully inspired Word of God, but rather it *contains* God's Word.[8] Many of its teachings are reflective not of God's view of things but the culturally conditioned views of the people who wrote it. Thus, not all the teachings of the Bible are entirely trustworthy.[9] Therefore, if we want to live in a way that honors God, we have to judge Scripture by some other authority. What we think about sexual ethics is an issue that reveals this practice. What is our authority to determine the rightness or wrongness of sexual acts? It seems, for this progressive pastor, that his moral intuition (often triggered by stories of individuals hurt by the church) and the insights of science (as it relates to human psychology and sexuality) are better guides than Scripture. New Testament scholar Luke Timothy Johnson expresses a similar view:

> I have little patience with efforts to make Scripture say something other than what it says, through appeals to linguistic or cultural subtleties. The exegetical situation is straightforward: we know what the text says. . . .
>
> I think it important to state clearly that we do, in fact, reject the straightforward commands of Scripture, and appeal instead to another authority when we declare that same-sex unions can be holy and good. And what exactly is that authority? We appeal explicitly to the weight of our own experience and the experience thousands of others have witnessed to, which tells us that to claim our own sexual orientation is in fact to accept the way in which God has created us.[10]

According to this view, Scripture is neither entirely trustworthy nor ultimately authoritative. At best, it is a fallible guide that offers a mixture of truth and error and must be judged by a higher authority. As Professor Johnson says, when something the Bible teaches doesn't align with the "the weight of our own experience and the experience [of] thousands of others," we should reject it. Although progressive Christians may differ on what authorities they appeal to in interpreting the Bible, they agree that Scripture must bow to higher authority.

Why the Difference?

If the historic view of the Bible is that it is entirely trustworthy in all that it teaches, why have some contemporary believers chosen a different view? The answer to that question is complex and would involve a deep dive into the history of thought and critical scholarship, but that would take us far afield of the purpose of this chapter. However, the idea that we ought to question the Bible's authority is due in large measure to the fact that some of what the Bible records, and appears to teach, strikes modern readers as morally problematic. Whether it's the violence of the Old Testament or the restrictive view of sexuality in the New Testament, there's plenty to make us wonder if God is really behind such seemingly morally problematic commands. Many ask honest questions such as:

God explicitly commanded Joshua to wipe out all the Canaanites. But isn't it self-evident that killing innocent Canaanite women and children is wrong?

Can it really be the case that Jesus—who is God—in the New Testament commanded us to love our enemies but in the Old Testament commanded the Israelites to destroy theirs?

What is more likely, that God commanded disobedient children be stoned to death or that Moses was mistaken and projected his barbaric cultural views onto God?

Would God really limit certain leadership roles in the church based on gender?

Isn't hell incompatible with the love of God?

One way to resolve these tensions is to believe that the authors of Scripture got God wrong. The authors, not God, are responsible for these bad teachings. God may have allowed mistaken beliefs to be attributed to him in Scripture, but he does not support them. Thus, we are under no compulsion to accept all of it as divinely inspired and authoritative. On this view, we *ought* to reject some of it in obedience to Jesus.

Why the Progressive View Fails

As you might guess, we side with the historic Christian view that the Bible is inspired by God in its entirety. Our reasons for holding that view aren't simply because we prefer it. To be honest, there are times when the progressive views seem appealing to us. We understand the tensions mentioned and have wrestled deeply with them. Furthermore, Scripture has some hard teachings that make us feel both uncomfortable and convicted. It's tempting to say those teachings aren't reflective of God. But ultimately, we resist the temptation to adopt the progressive view for the following reasons.

First, as we have stated, there is a clear consensus throughout the history of the church regarding the nature of Scripture. The consensus view has been that the Bible is both authoritative and trustworthy in all that it affirms.[11] To adopt a different view of Scripture than that of Irenaeus, Justin Martyr, Clement of Alexandria, Cyprian, Athanasius, Augustine, Jerome, Aquinas, Luther, Calvin, Whitefield, and Edwards seems unwise. Before rejecting the consensus position of the church on the nature of Scripture, we would need very persuasive arguments for doing so.

Second, Jesus viewed the Old Testament as inspired and authoritative. He frequently referred to individuals and historical events as if he believed they existed and occurred. Jesus refers to over thirty individuals or events in the Old Testament as historically real, including ones in many of the very passages that make modern readers uncomfortable.[12] Jesus also recognized the Old Testament as the final authority in matters of faith and practice when he contended with the religious leaders. Jesus didn't appeal to other rabbis or current traditions but to himself or the Old Testament to make his point. For example, the Sadducees (a religious sect that didn't believe in the resurrection) tried to make Jesus look foolish by presenting him with a scenario that would seemingly undermine his teaching on the resurrection. Jesus responded by telling them the reason they were wrong was because they didn't know the Scriptures. In his defense, Jesus quoted from the book of Exodus (Matt. 22:23–33). In religious debates, Jesus regularly appealed to the Old Testament as the final arbiter of truth.

Jesus had such a high view of the Old Testament that, in one passage, he ascribes to God a comment made by the author of Genesis. In Matthew 19:4–5 Jesus is discussing marriage and divorce with the religious leaders. He refers to Genesis 2:24 to make his case, but instead of saying "as the Scripture says" or "as Moses says" (which would have been the most natural way of citing that passage), Jesus put it this way: "At the beginning the Creator 'made them male and female,' and said, 'For this reason a man will leave his father and mother and be united to his wife, and the two will become one flesh'" (Matt. 19:4 NIV). Technically speaking, the writer of Genesis wrote these words, yet Jesus attributes them to God himself! This shows how high a view Jesus had of the Old Testament.[13] For Jesus, the Old Testament was nothing less than God's word.

Third, whatever standard is adopted to discern the true from the false in Scripture becomes the authority that stands above Scripture. But just what criterion is worthy of such a lofty role? For the progressive view, the criteria include experience, science, or moral intuition. But each of these is highly problematic as an ultimate authority. The findings of science change, experiences differ from person to person, and all kinds of factors shape moral intuition. In other words, they are far too subjective and error-prone to stand in judgment of the Bible.

Some progressive Christians see the unreliability of the previous options and choose to consider Jesus as the lens through which we can judge the Bible. In practical terms, this means that if a biblical claim doesn't line up with our understanding of Jesus, we should reject it. The rationale for using Jesus as the criterion is as follows. Scripture tells us that in the past God spoke to his people by way of prophets, but in these last days he has spoken to us by his Son (Heb. 1:1–2). Jesus is more than a prophet. He is the express image of God himself (Col. 1:15–16), which makes him God's clearest revelation of himself to humanity. Therefore, we ought to evaluate the Bible through the lens of Jesus. If we can't see Jesus endorsing a particular teaching or giving a specific command, we have good reason to believe that part of the Bible doesn't come from God but is rather the mistaken view of the human author.

What could possibly be wrong with a view that seems to elevate Jesus so highly?[14] We can think of at least five things. To begin with, it assumes a view of Scripture we reject. According to this view, Jesus is needed as a higher authority because of the assumption that the Bible isn't trustworthy. We ask, Why start with this assumption?

Second, as we've seen, Jesus confirmed some of the Bible's most offensive passages. Jesus believed God flooded the entire world (killing all but Noah and his family) and destroyed Sodom and Gomorrah with fire and brimstone. He affirmed the entire Mosaic law with all its harsh penalties (including stoning and maiming).[15]

Third, it ignores Jesus's teaching about himself as a righteous judge who will say to some, "Depart from me, you cursed, into the eternal fire prepared for the devil and his angels."[16] This is a terrifying image and one that should give us pause. Jesus tells us that although he is a gracious and loving savior, he is also a righteous judge. Too often those who view Scripture through the "Jesus lens" do not appreciate this aspect of Jesus.

Fourth, it ignores the teaching of the apostles. In 2 Thessalonians, Jesus is depicted as executing God's justice by "inflicting vengeance on those who do not know God and on those who do not obey the gospel of our Lord Jesus. They will suffer the punishment of eternal destruction" (2 Thess. 1:8–9). The apostle John, in the book of Revelation, describes the scene when Jesus returns to defeat the Beast and his followers. We include the entire section because it stands in such stark contrast to the Jesus of the Jesus lens.

> I saw heaven standing open and there before me was a white horse, whose rider is called Faithful and True. With justice he judges and wages war. His eyes are like blazing fire, and on his head are many crowns. He has a name written on him that no one knows but he himself. He is dressed in a robe dipped in blood, and his name is the Word of God. The armies of heaven were following him, riding on white horses and dressed in fine linen, white and clean. Coming out of his mouth is a sharp sword with which to strike down the nations. "He will rule them with an iron scepter." He treads the winepress of the fury of the wrath of God Almighty.[17]

These are undoubtedly difficult teachings. But if Jesus didn't shy away from affirming the entire word of God—including the difficult parts—then as his disciples we ought to follow his example, trusting that he knows better than we do.

Fifth and finally, the Jesus lens is often employed only to *avoid* that which offends us. Those who adjudicate Scripture through the lens of Jesus never seem to see God as more wrathful, more intolerant, or more exclusive. On the contrary, the Jesus lens seems to coincidentally align with the values of contemporary culture. Shouldn't that give us pause? We think so, because it severely limits the Bible's ability to do its job, which is to correct *our* mistaken beliefs. How so? When Scripture runs afoul of our values, or those of what Paul calls the "world," then Scripture's values, rather the world's values, will be seen as the problem. If that happens, how can Scripture do its job of correcting and teaching us (2 Tim. 3:16)? It can't, at least not as it was intended to.

What's Your View?

We began this chapter by challenging you to consider how your assumptions about the Bible set the trajectory of your deconstruction. Hopefully, now you can see why. Because of the centrality of the Bible to the Christian life, the view of Scripture you adopt will powerfully shape your understanding of how to follow Jesus. To use this chapter's initial illustration, your assumptions about the nature of Scripture will be the coordinates from which you determine the direction of your deconstruction.

If you embrace a view that allows you to reject parts of the Bible, there is a real danger that you will reconstruct a Christianity that reflects more of who you are than who Jesus is. That's because, as broken humans, most of us are tempted to reject the parts of the Bible that we don't like. A better set of coordinates to guide you back to the shore and a faithful Christian community is that of Jesus and the historic church, which is that the Bible is trustworthy and authoritative in everything it teaches.

By the way, are you wondering what voice Seaman Parker listened to as the German plane bore down on him and his fellow sailors? Fortunately, it was Lieutenant Tyler, his rightful authority. Had he listened to the voices telling him Tyler was untrustworthy, he would have fired on the plane and revealed to the clueless German pilot that they were Americans, which would have resulted in disaster.

Reflection Questions

1. After reading this chapter, which of the two versions we presented, the historic and progressive views of Scripture, are you more inclined toward? Why?

2. How important is your belief about the Bible in terms of the kind of Christian faith you adopt? How should we decide what to believe about the authority of the Bible?

3. The authors of the books of the Bible were influenced by their culture, worldview, and historical setting. Consequently, the books they authored have evidence of their historical situatedness all through them. Does this mean the authors got some things wrong? Why or why not?

4. What are your thoughts about using Jesus as a lens to determine which parts of the Old Testament are reflective of God and which parts are cultural distortions of the Israelites?

CHAPTER 6

Know Your Culture

I always felt called to . . . live and die for something bigger than yourself.

—Cornel West

Honoring your parents sounds great, but if you take it too far, well, you might forget to honor yourself. Luckily, I don't have that problem.

—Meilin Lee

Victor Hugo's novel *The Man Who Laughs*, describes a hideous practice: that of molding humans. Hugo writes that,

> In China, from time immemorial, they have possessed a certain . . . art. It is the art of molding a living man. They take a child, two or three years old, put him in a porcelain vase, more or less grotesque, which is made without top or bottom. . . . During the day the vase is set upright, and at night is laid down to allow the child to sleep. . . . This

development in a bottle continues many years. After a certain time it becomes irreparable. When they consider that this is accomplished, and the monster made, they break the vase.[1]

Why was such a horrific practice developed? For no other reason than the amusement of the nobles.[2]

The practice of molding humans does more than just illustrate how sinful humans are, it also illustrates how physically malleable we are. Given the right external forces and enough time, our bodies can be squeezed into unimaginable shapes. We're guessing, however, that having your body appallingly contorted probably isn't something you're too worried about. And for good reasons. You're no longer a toddler, and nobody is putting people in vases these days. And yet, like those tragic children, we too are being molded and shaped by forces beyond our control. Only it's not our bodies that are being molded, it's our minds. But unlike those children, we are often unaware such transformation is happening.

What's Water?

In 2005 David Foster Wallace, the celebrated American author, delivered the commencement address to the graduating class of Kenyon College. Wallace began his speech with the following parable: "There are these two young fish swimming along and they happen to meet an older fish swimming the other way, who nods at them and says, 'Morning, boys. How's the water?' And the two young fish swim on for a bit, and then eventually one of them looks over at the other and goes, 'What the hell is water?'"[3]

Wallace's fish tale echoes a much older Chinese proverb that says, "If you want to know how the water is, don't ask the fish." Like fish, we are immersed in environments that we're largely unaware of because they act as the very conditions for our existence. We don't realize we're in a kind of "water" that influences everything we think and do. Like fish, we take our experience as the natural order of things.

If we're being squeezed into a mental mold, then what is the mold? What is the "water" we're unaware of? Many influencing forces are at work in our lives. Part of finding our way out of the fog and back to shore is to become aware of how those forces have influenced our beliefs, affections, and attitudes. It's important to realize that much of what we believe is a result of various factors and only *one* of them is our conscious reasoning process. Other factors beyond our conscious awareness are also at play, and that's what makes them so influential and potentially dangerous.

One of the most powerful and imperceptible forces that shape our beliefs and values is our *social imaginary*. If we really want to understand the impulse to deconstruct, we need to understand both what social imaginaries are and what our particular social imaginary is. Like the largest part of an iceberg, the social imaginary often lies below the surface of our awareness.

The goal of this chapter is to help bring clarity about the "water" that often imperceptibly surrounds us and to help us recognize how it fosters the urge to deconstruct. To some degree, we all feel the impulse to rethink, evaluate, and question what we're told we must believe. As we have said many times in this book, questioning and evaluating are *good* things, and we encourage them! But where does the modern urge to deconstruct come from? Why are so many people feeling this urge in such a pressing manner today? We want to suggest that something deep is going on. All of us are "swimming" in cultural waters we often miss. Please stay with us in this chapter. We're going deep! But we believe the payoff will be significant.

Imagine That!

Social imaginaries aren't easy to define. But simply put, they're the way people *imagine*, not think about, their social surroundings. Social imaginaries aren't primarily philosophies of life, but rather shared assumptions and background conditions that societies are built on. All social imaginaries contain an unspoken vision of how the world (in general) and people (in particular) ought to be. They reflect how we *assume* the world is prior to *thinking* about it. Social imaginaries influence us by shaping the deepest parts of our hearts.[4] They quietly go about their work by influencing our intuitions and moral sensibilities. In turn, they influence our conscious reasoning processes. Because we don't adopt them by way of conscious evaluation but absorb them by osmosis, they're hard to detect. But one thing is certain: they squeeze us into their mold without our awareness.

Let's consider an example. I (John) recently spoke to a group of high school and college students at a church in Southern California. Afterward, a student asked if we could talk. He wanted my opinion on LGBTQ relationships. Wanting to know how to answer him well, I asked if he would mind telling me what he thought about the issue. He said, "I believe the Bible is God's Word. And I believe up here [pointing to his head] that it teaches that homosexuality is not God's intention for people and that same-sex intercourse is sin." Then he pointed to his heart and said, "But I just can't shake the feeling that it would be wrong for two people who love each other to be denied the opportunity to express that love toward each other. I *believe* it's wrong, but I *feel* that it's not."

Notice he didn't give me *reasons* why he felt that same-sex practices are okay. The best he could offer was saying that in his heart he didn't feel that same-sex practices were wrong. Why did he feel that way? Because of his social imaginary. Had he lived one hundred years ago, he would've both *believed* and *felt* same-sex unions were wrong. Because one hundred years ago he would've indwelled a different social imaginary. He wouldn't even have asked his question because it would never have occurred to him. On this issue, one hundred years ago, there wouldn't have been any tension between his beliefs and his feelings. Today, because of our different social imaginary, many of us feel tension between what we believe and what we feel on a variety of issues.

Compare and Contrast

If social imaginaries play such a formative role in how we conceive the world, then it's important to understand the social imaginary we live in, or better yet, which lives in us. The best way to do that is by contrasting our social imaginary with another one. Doing so can help bring ours into clearer focus.

The social imaginary that preceded our own goes by various names, but we're going to call it the age of obligation.[5] The age of obligation, which lasted from the beginning of the twentieth century through the 1950s, was characterized by a deep sense of obligation.[6] Journalist Tom Brokaw named those who embodied the age of obligation as "The Greatest Generation." Born between 1901 and 1927, the Greatest Generation liberated Europe from the Nazis and then returned home and built America into the world's greatest superpower. Brokaw argues that the reason they accomplished those two incredible feats was because of the values instilled in them by their social imaginary.[7] Brokaw identified those values as personal responsibility, duty, honor, and faith.[8]

An important assumption of the age of obligation was that there was a given order to reality that could be discovered through reflection and observation. A second assumption was that each person had a duty to align oneself with reality. A third assumption was that the values of the Unites States largely reflected the values of reality.[9] Therefore, individuals were duty-bound to a vision of the world they assumed reflected the nature of reality. Responsibility, duty, honor, and faith were owed to something bigger than individual desire.

To see this, consider the military draft of World War II. Even though there was a draft for the war, it wasn't the power of the government that put men in uniforms; they were motivated to fight because of their sense of duty and responsibility to something greater than themselves.[10] To enlist in the military only because one was forced to by the government would have been shameful for members of the Greatest Generation.[11] Contrast that with the response of American youth during the Vietnam War only twenty years later. When the United States enacted the draft for Vietnam, the response of Americans to "do their duty" was met with resistance. Draft cards and bras were burned, protests took place, and some even defected rather than fight.[12]

These anti-war feelings were part of a larger counterculture movement that defined the 1960s and 1970s. Inspired by a distrust of "the establishment," young people challenged the long-standing social norms they were expected to uphold. They looked for freedom from institutions, systems, and ideologies because they no longer saw them as reflecting the values of reality but the values of the powerful.

What brought about the change in attitude from the dutiful youth of the 1940s to the activists of the 1960s? According to theologian Andrew Root, "What ignited the flames of rebellion in the 1960s, as much as matches, was the arrival of authenticity—the idea that your own path, your own desires and wishes, must lead you before any duty or obligation."[13] As the 1960s came to an end, a new era dawned.

We now live in what can be described as the age of authenticity.[14] In this age, the first and (maybe) only obligation you have is to be authentically yourself. What matters in the age of authenticity is expressing who you are, speaking your truth, and not conforming to the expectations, roles, or identities placed on you by anybody else's vision of the world. Philosopher Charles Taylor defined the age of authenticity this way: "Each one of us has his/her own way of realizing our humanity, and that it is important to find and live out one's own, as against surrendering to conformity with a model imposed on us from outside, by society, or the previous generation, or religious or political authority."[15]

Or, as people often say, "You do you."

Shifting Sands

What brought about this radical change in attitude from the age of obligation to the age of authenticity? Several factors played a role, but one stands out as particularly significant: the change in what we think about knowledge.[16] In the age of obligation, it was taken for granted that there was an objective reality that could be known. But those living in the age of authenticity question this assumption. Rather than a focus on knowledge, the focus has shifted to suspicion and skepticism concerning knowledge.

We've become highly sensitive to factors that those in the age of obligation were largely unaware of. One of those is what is sometimes called our situatedness. Our unique situations (for example, the language we speak, our culture, our gender, and our ethnicity) impact how we see reality. Even more, they supposedly hinder us from seeing reality *as it is*. They act as lenses through which we view the world. But these lenses distort what we see. Worse, we can never take them off to confirm whether our view matches up with reality. Consequently, no one can know reality *as it is*. We only ever have competing interpretations and experiences of it.

Recognizing the current skepticism about knowledge can help us see how the shift has occurred from the age of obligation to the age of authenticity. The age of obligation assumed reality had an objective structure that was reflected in the social norms of society. Therefore, individuals ought to conform themselves to it both for their well-being and for the sake of the societal good. Consequently, personal responsibility, duty, honor, and faith to something greater than oneself were values that were at home in the age of obligation.

In the age of authenticity, on the other hand, either there isn't a natural order of things or, if there is one, we can't know it. All we have are competing social constructs. A social construct is a set of shared ideas about society that exists only because a group of people agree on them. Social constructions are sometimes mistaken by the group as reflecting reality itself. For example, the idea that blue is masculine and pink is feminine is a social construct. Pink could easily have been associated with boys and blue with girls (as it has in the past). A color tied to a sex is not a feature of reality but of our construction of reality. But try telling that to a seven-year-old boy! For him, the social construct of reality has merged with reality itself.

In the age of authenticity, most, if not all, significant matters are social constructs. The long-held understanding of marriage, gender, sexuality, family, and the self are viewed as nothing more than social constructs. This shift in the social imaginary leads to the following kinds of questions:

- Who says marriage is only between one man and one woman and not a thruple?[17]
- Who says that pornography is immoral and not artistic expression?

- Who says the ideals of America are noble and not oppressive?
- Who says I can't choose to end my life on my terms as opposed to suffering?
- Who says that my gender expression ought to align with my biological sex?

Once we lose the belief that reality can be known, we naturally lose any sense of obligation to anything beyond the self. In the age of authenticity, the only sense of responsibility, duty, honor, and faith an individual experiences is to their own values, beliefs, and identity. Conforming to the expectations of others makes little sense. If reality is entirely socially constructed, why would I have an obligation to conform myself to its demands? On the contrary, I *ought* to throw off the confines of the construct that limits me expressing myself. In the words of Post Malone, "I'm gonna be what I want, what I want, what I want, yeah (yeah)."[18]

For Malone and many others today, there's no good reason *not* to pursue "my truth" by living however I want.

Express Yourself

Since we've been so shaped by the age of authenticity, we might have a hard time seeing how it manifests itself. Consider three ways that the right to express oneself has impacted our understanding of the world.

#1: MARRIAGE AND THE PURSUIT OF HAPPINESS

The first is that we prioritize individual rights over the responsibilities and duties we have toward others. Pursuing our individual rights is the ultimate path to personal happiness. When the pursuit of each person's happiness is no longer connected to, or limited by, a larger shared vision of the world as it was in the age of obligation, social obligations lose their force. If there isn't a shared vision of the good that demands our allegiance, then we're left with only personal preferences about what *we feel* is good. This change from a larger shared vision to one of personal happiness as our guiding star has altered the way we understand long-standing cultural institutions. Consider no-fault divorce.

In the West, the family has been considered the foundational relationship of society. It is both a personal and public institution that contributes to the good of its members and to society. Getting married and having children encourages men to grow up. It allows women the security to become mothers. It tames destructive male instincts. Married men are less likely to join gangs, deal drugs, and commit random violence. They get jobs and become productive members of their communities.[19] And children who live with two parents do better in school, are better adjusted, and are more likely to avoid destructive behavior.[20] All of this explains why the state was interested in the success of marriages and why it discouraged divorce. As a result, there had to be something that violated or did irreparable damage to the marriage to dissolve it. Being unhappy didn't cut it. Well, until 1969.

In 1969 California adopted the United States' first no-fault divorce law. No-fault divorce doesn't require the spouse seeking the divorce to show that their partner violated the marriage covenant. All that matters is that one person in the marriage no longer *wants* to be married. The reason for the shift in requirements reflects the shift in the view of marriage.[21] It's true that previous generations would have recognized that marriage can bring about personal fulfillment, but that wasn't the *primary* reason people got married. Security, survival, having and raising children, economic stability, and social alliances all played vital roles. In entering a marriage, each person recognized obligations that were to come before their personal happiness. Minimally, marriage entailed a commitment to ensure the well-being of one's children.

In the age of authenticity, this all changes. Marriage is viewed as an arrangement that exists almost exclusively to achieve personal fulfillment, with no further obligations. Thus, if a person isn't fulfilled in their marriage, they should get a divorce. Not doing so would sacrifice their own happiness. A tragic example of this is the singer Adele, who ended her marriage in pursuit of her own happiness even though it cost her young son his.

> It just wasn't right for me anymore. I didn't want to end up like a lot of other people I knew. I wasn't *miserable* miserable, but I would have been miserable had I not put myself first.[22]

> If I can reach the reason why I left, which was the pursuit of my own happiness, even though it made Angelo [her son] really unhappy—if I can find that happiness and he sees me in that happiness, then maybe I'll be able to forgive myself for it.[23]

> I voluntarily chose to dismantle his [her son's] entire life in the pursuit of my own happiness. It made him really unhappy sometimes.[24]

Our hearts break for him.

#2: SEX AND GENDER

The second and most obvious way that the drive for authenticity manifests is in how we think about sexuality and gender. While it was once assumed that a person's gender was determined by one's biology, that's no longer the case. Now many people assume that gender is determined by a subjective inner sense. Again, we see the shift away from finding truth in an external, objective reality to the focus on an internal, subjective sense that must be followed to bring happiness.

This is a powerful expression of individualism. People are encouraged not only to deconstruct systems that come from *without* but also to do the same to my very self *within*. People should not be forced to adopt an "arbitrary gender" that comes from a social construct, especially if doing so detracts from their own happiness. In the age of authenticity, people's allegiance is to psychological well-being, not objective reality. Consider pop star Demi Lovato, who in 2021 identified as nonbinary: "I feel that this best represents the fluidity I feel in my gender expression and allows me to feel most authentic and true to the person I both know I am, and am still discovering."[25] Referring to a drug overdose that occurred in 2018, Lovato said, "In 2018 when I overdosed, I feel like the reason why that happened was because I was ignoring my truth, and I was suppressing who I really am. . . . I just realize that it's so much more important to live your truth than to ever suppress yourself because that's the type of stuff that happens when you do."[26]

But aren't there times when living "your truth" might be unwise? Aren't there parts of us that we should suppress? Aren't there some things more important than being true to yourself? Not in the age of authenticity.

#3: Institutions

Third, we no longer see institutions, such as the university or the church, as a means of character and behavior formation that we submit to, but as stages on which we perform and display ourselves to the world.[27] This need to perform and display ourselves is easy to see in the world of social media, which is designed primarily for self-expression. Platforms such as YouTube, TikTok, and Instagram are, as journalist Brett McCracken puts it, spaces "for public affirmation, not private growth; virtue-signaling more than virtue cultivation."[28] He goes on to argue that it was once expected of individuals that they would adapt to the institution they joined, but "now, the burden of belonging falls squarely on the institution. If a member feels unappreciated, alienated, or unseen, it's the *institution's* responsibility to make that individual feel they belong—not at all the other way around."[29] The individual's feelings, not the institution's, reign supreme.

At Oklahoma Wesleyan University, a student complained to the administration that he was made to feel unsafe and victimized by a sermon delivered in chapel. The sermon on 1 Corinthians 13, Paul's famous passage on love, made him feel uncomfortable for being unloving. He argued that the university should have given a trigger warning that the sermon might make some students uncomfortable. By not doing so, it had victimized him and others. For this student, the university wasn't an institution he attended to be shaped and molded into its values. Rather, it was a platform to express his values and be his authentic self. For him, his time there was not to be formed by the university, but for the university to conform to him.[30]

To be clear, we're not condemning Adele, Demi Lovato, or the student at Oklahoma Wesleyan. We love Adele's music, cheer for Demi in her life, and assume the student at OWU is a genuinely nice guy. We'd love to hang out with all of them if we could. We highlight them not to pick on them but because they offer such clear examples of how we are all formed by the waters of our social imaginary. This is true for all of us.

What's Your Point?

What does all this talk about social imaginaries and the age of authenticity have to do with deconstructing one's faith? Let's make it explicit. Our goal in this chapter was to raise awareness of the water in which we swim and how it forms us. That water is our present social imaginary, which we have called the age of authenticity. It instills in us the belief that being true to ourselves is our greatest obligation. As a result, the greatest sin is to be inauthentic. It's *this* impulse—the need to be authentic— that plays a huge role in deconstruction. Theologian Andrew Root laments that in the age of authenticity, "to deconstruct faith becomes the ultimate act of authenticity."[31]

Realizing this can help us as we reconsider our beliefs. This urge makes deconstruction seem like not only the natural thing to do but also *a moral imperative*. And only when we're aware of it can we be discerning of how and why we deconstruct. Rather than simply following the push to be authentic, we can reflect on this urge itself and respond with intentionality.

It's important to realize that this approach to faith formation (individual deconstruction) hasn't been the norm throughout the history of the church. While there are some notable exceptions, the average Christian wouldn't have thought to deconstruct their faith. This is a unique characteristic of our age. The reason they wouldn't was because they weren't motivated by the need to express their authenticity. They didn't have the same individualistic impulse that we do today. They were more concerned with conforming to the expectations and standards imposed on them (which they thought reflected the nature of reality) than they were in "living their truth." To be sure, unquestioningly accepting the norm out of a sense of duty is just as bad as challenging the norm because one feels the need for authenticity. God has made you with unique abilities, characteristics, and desires. We are all special individuals who should be celebrated. But we also have duties to people and institutions outside of ourselves. All of us have a duty to seek truth and to conform our lives to it even when it may not personally feel good.

The problem isn't in accepting what you have been taught or rethinking what you've been taught, it's *why* you're doing it. Is it because the faith you've received doesn't ring true to "who you are"? Is it because it doesn't meet your values? Does it fail to meet your needs? Does it hinder you from finding your personal happiness? Is it motivated by the desire to be free from expectations and regulations of your parents or your church?[32] If the answer to any of these questions is yes, then your motivation to deconstruct may have been influenced by unhealthy and hidden aspects of our culture. If it's driven by a deep desire to be in the truth, that's very different.

Every age has its own "water." The apostle Paul knew this. He also knew how easy it is to be conformed to it without awareness. Therefore, he warned Christians in Rome to be on guard against the elements of their age that were harmful to their faith: "Do not be conformed to this world, but be transformed by the renewal of your mind, that by testing you may discern what is the will of God, what is good and acceptable and perfect" (Rom. 12:2).

Notice, Paul warned them about being "conformed" to this world. Our natural tendency is to passively conform to the world around us. Paul wanted the Christians in Rome to be aware of the "world" they were immersed in so they could resist being molded to it, much like the vases molded the bodies of the young children in Hugo's novel.

As you paddle toward the shore, be aware of and resist being squeezed into the "worldly" aspects of our social imaginary. The age of authenticity instills in us an impulse to deconstruct and reconstruct the Christian faith in a way that is little more than a reflection of internal feelings and desires.

This impulse acts like an ocean current that subtly pulls us out to the open sea and deeper into the fog by compelling us to reject any part of the Bible that doesn't feel authentic and doesn't align with our values. It tempts us to reinterpret Scripture to avoid teachings we don't like. If we aren't intentional about being transformed by the renewing of our minds, as Paul instructs, then the faith we reconstruct can become as deformed as the bodies of the children in the porcelain vases.

Reflection Questions

1. Do you agree that culture can deeply shape our beliefs? Why or why not?

2. Can you think of any examples from movies, the internet, advertising, etc. that reinforce the idea that being "authentically you" is of primary importance?

3. Do you think the idea of the age of authenticity accurately describes our cultural moment? If so, how might we resist the pressure to seek "authenticity" in unhealthy ways?

4. Did a part of you resonate with Adele, Demi, and the college student? If so, what might that reveal about how you have been formed by the culture?

5. How much of deconstruction is driven by the felt need young Christians have to be authentic to themselves? Is that a good reason to deconstruct?

CHAPTER 7

Know Yourself

There are three things extremely hard:
steel, a diamond, and to know one's self.
—BENJAMIN FRANKLIN

The way that I sing, what I sing
about, what I wear, who I am, this
is me. I was born this way.
—LADY GAGA

Kate is an intelligent and reflective twenty-one-year-old college sophomore. Politically, she leans left on most issues. She supports candidates who prioritize fighting for equality and caring for the needy. On her campus, Kate is a leader in the racial reconciliation club, which seeks to bring awareness to the presence of racism in society. Kate's appearance falls somewhere between grunge and steampunk. Her brown hair is shaved almost to the scalp, and her right eyebrow is pierced with a hoop in it. She usually wears black Doc Martens and black jeans. On her left wrist is a tattoo that simply says "Love."

Kate identifies as a Christian. A serious one. She believes that everyone, regardless of their faith, sexual orientation, gender, or immigration status deserves to be treated with dignity and respect.

Kate's concern for social justice stems from her faith in Jesus. The church she goes to is solidly within the historic Christian faith, but its emphasis is, according to Kate, "less on preaching and more on doing." But she hasn't always been this way. Her boyfriend wouldn't recognize her if he saw a picture of her at fifteen years old. Her parents hardly recognize her today.

Growing up as the firstborn in a Christian family, Kate was conscientious, dutiful, and had a strong desire to do what is right. That desire led her to adopt the perspective of her parents and church on everything from theology to politics. She took strong stands on issues traditionally identified with the right side of the political spectrum, believing they mirrored what the Bible taught. Back then it was important for her to avoid non-Christians unless she was evangelizing them, lest they taint her with their sin. At fifteen, Kate dressed modestly compared with other girls her age and wore her long brown hair parted in the middle. She didn't wear jewelry because she believed it was inappropriate to draw attention to herself. But she made one exception—a purity ring she received when she was fourteen.

You might be wondering what happened to Kate to cause such a change. Her family and church definitely are! If you are in the process of deconstructing right now, it's possible that what happened to Kate is also happening to you. Perhaps, like Kate, you are finally discovering who you really are.

In this chapter, we want to highlight one significant factor that causes Christians to rethink what it means to be a follower of Jesus. We hope to make sense of why you also may find yourself on this journey. Knowing who you are, and what you value, can help you to identify a Christian community you can begin paddling toward.

Who Am I?

In the movie *The Nanny Diaries*, Annie Braddock, a recent college graduate, finds herself interviewing for an internship with a big corporation. After informing Annie of how strong the competition for the internship is, the high-powered corporate executive asks Annie her first question. It is a softball.

"So, why don't you tell me in your own words, who exactly is Annie Braddock?"

Relieved to begin with such an easy question, Annie jumps right in. "Well, that's certainly an easy enough question." But instead of hitting that question out of the park, she swings and misses. After starting to answer the question, Annie becomes confused, stammers, pauses, and then blurts out, "Annie Braddock is . . . I have absolutely no idea."

With that, she jumps up and runs out of the office. When the next scene cuts to Annie as she is walking along the city street, we hear her inner thoughts as a voice-over. "Who is Annie Braddock? It wasn't exactly a trick question. Yet somehow I couldn't formulate a response. Of course, I knew all the basic facts—date of birth, hometown, socioeconomic makeup. But I didn't really know who I was, where I fit in, who I was gonna be. I was suddenly terrified I would never find the answer."[1]

For a lot of Christians, deconstruction begins with an experience like Annie's. Something triggers them to wake up to the fact that they don't know who they are. Like Annie, they know the basics: date of birth, hometown, etc. But for one reason or another, they realize they've never thought deeply about *what* they believe and *why* they believe it. This happens because most Christians grow up into a version of Christianity they simply assume is true. Maybe it was a version that placed great emphasis on having correct beliefs. Maybe it highly valued holy living and separation from the world. It may have been a faith that was primarily experiential. Or it could have been a tradition that prized social justice and political action. Regardless of what version of the faith they find themselves in, everyone who begins the deconstruction journey has a moment when they ask themselves, "Is this who I really am?" If the answer is no, the next question is, "Then who am I?" At least that's the question Kate asked.

At twenty-one, Kate realized she wasn't the person she and everyone else always thought she was. Her conscientious, pleasing, and dutiful nature conformed itself to the beliefs of her parents and church community. Wanting to honor God and her parents, Kate did what they said and believed what they believed. And it all seemed right to her. So what changed? Kate grew up.

Psychologists tell us that in childhood we unconsciously alter our behavior and repress feelings or beliefs to fit in with those from whom we most desire acceptance (for example, family, role models). One way we do that is by adopting and affirming the beliefs and practices that are most important to them. But, over time, as we grow in our self-confidence and self-identity, the need for that acceptance lessens. When that happens, the true personal beliefs and feelings emerge.

As she grew up, Kate became increasingly aware that her beliefs and identity didn't match up with her community's as seamlessly as they had before. Eventually, living out the version of the faith she was raised with felt like a straitjacket. Feeling guilty, she tried to bring her changing perspective in line with that of her parents and church community, but as time passed it was like trying to keep a beachball submerged underwater. Her life felt unnatural and forced.

Kate's story raises the question of why we believe some of the things we do. Why is it that beliefs we feel passionately about sometimes differ from those of our parents or church community? In the next section we'll present one major reason why that happens. But be aware: to do so, we're going to trigger your moral intuitions.

We Know What Before We Know Why

We are going to ask you a few questions for reflection. First, do you think it is wrong for two people of the opposite sex to passionately kiss each other? Does your answer change if you discover that those two people are brother and sister? We suspect that even if you had some qualifications about the first question (as long as they're married, engaged, in a long-term relationship, etc.), you probably have no problem, in principle, with people of the opposite sex kissing passionately.

On the other hand, we strongly suspect that your answer to the second question was an emphatic, "Yes, it's absolutely wrong for them to do that. It's also gross and deeply disturbing!" But why do you believe that? What are your reasons? Take a minute and list the reasons you'd give for your belief. You might find it harder to do than you first imagine. If both are consenting adults, who does it hurt? It doesn't break any laws. Maybe you think it could strengthen their sibling bond. So why is it wrong? What are your reasons?

For the record, we agree that passionate kissing between siblings is morally wrong and disturbing. But we ask the question to highlight the role that intuition plays in decision-making. If you believe it's wrong for siblings to make out with each other, you did not reason your way to that conclusion. It was another cognitive process, known as intuition, that formed that belief. Your strategic reasoning kicked in *after* you knew it was wrong—you knew what you believed before you knew why. In other words, your reasoning was the caboose, not the train engine.

Intuition is a mental ability that forms beliefs instantaneously, without deliberation, and makes them feel obvious to us. Many of our beliefs are the result of intuition. For example, if you're told, "Water is wet" you don't need to hear an argument for why that's true. You intuitively understand that it must be. If asked why you believe it's true, you could muster some reasons, but those reasons aren't the basis of your belief, your intuition is. You could just "see" the truth of the claim. It was self-evident.

One significant role of intuition is to form our moral beliefs. Moral intuition just "sees" or "feels" that some things are wrong even before we give them conscious thought or reflection. Again, through our moral intuition, we know siblings passionately kissing each other is wrong before we even think about it. The idea of moral intuition and the role it plays in belief formation come from the work of Jonathan Haidt, a moral psychologist at New York University. He has demonstrated that we affirm or deny a moral claim not through reasoning but by whether it triggers our moral intuition.

When we're forming beliefs about moral issues, conscious reasoning comes *after* our moral intuition has reached a conclusion. Our reason justifies the belief formed through intuition. It rationalizes it. It can also fool us into believing that we have arrived at our belief through a careful, conscious intellectual process. In reality, we arrive at our belief instantaneously and *then* come up with reasons to explain that belief to others, and maybe even ourselves.[2]

If intuition determines what we believe about moral

claims, we need to ask a deeper question: What guides our intuition?[3] If intuition is the engine that gets us to the destination of our beliefs (for example, it's wrong for siblings to kiss), what's driving the train? The answer is our values. Our greatest values determine our destination.[4] That is how people with different values can arrive at very different beliefs on the same issue.

Value Judgment

One of the most powerful forces that shapes how we perceive what it means to follow Jesus is our values. The values we honor most, more than any other factor, determine what we believe and how we live. In the deconstruction journey, realizing one's values (real values, not those we think we hold) is the catalyst for deconstructing. Values are the criteria we use to evaluate situations like kissing siblings.

Science tells us that human tongues have five taste receptors: sweet, salty, sour, bitter, and savory. And while each of us experiences those various tastes, we don't all appreciate them in the same way. Some people love sweet foods, whereas others prefer bitter ones. Some folks like savory dishes, others crave salty ones. Jonathan Haidt argues that, similar to our taste receptors, humans also share a moral foundation of six value and vice pairings that direct our moral intuition. Those value pairings are as follows:

- freedom / oppression
- care / harm
- fairness / cheating
- loyalty / betrayal
- authority / subversion
- sanctity / degradation

Haidt's research shows that humans universally believe the following about these six pairings. Freedom is good and oppression is bad. We ought to care for others and not do them harm. Fairness is right and cheating is wrong. Loyalty is a virtue to be praised and betrayal to be condemned. Legitimate authority should be respected and subverting it for illegitimate reasons is wrong. Some things are sacred, others are not.

Interestingly, Haidt points out a similarity between our taste receptors and our value and vice parings: although these six pairings make up our moral foundation, as with our taste receptors, we don't give them all equal weight. Some people value care more highly than freedom, and others esteem freedom more highly than care. For others, the most important value is loyalty, and so on. What happens when two people who differ in how they prioritize their values are faced with an issue that has moral implications? Even if they don't realize it, they come to different conclusions because their moral intuition follows their own hierarchy of values.

Consider the following situation.

Cody and Moriah are friends who share a lot in common. They're both Christians from middle-class homes and enjoy movies, play sports, and love traveling. They also want to serve Jesus by serving others, which has motivated them to start a ministry together. But there's one problem: they can't agree on what the ministry should be. Moriah suggests they care for individuals who have crossed the border illegally and are now homeless because they can't find work. Cody disagrees. He thinks that would be rewarding people who cheat the system. Each offers the other person reasons why their view is better. But it wasn't reason that brought them to belief, rather it was their moral intuition guided by how they weigh their values. Moriah prioritizes the value of *care*. She gives greater weight to caring for the suffering than she does the other five values.

Cody values *fairness* more than the other five. To him, caring for those who have broken the law seems unfair to those who entered the country legally who may be struggling financially. Moriah is unwilling to work with Cody because he discriminates in whom he's willing to care for. Cody is unwilling to work with Moriah because he feels cheaters shouldn't prosper. Neither of them will compromise their conviction and both are frustrated.

Are either of them right or wrong in how they *feel*? These kinds of situations are remarkably complex. Cody is correct: it's not fair. But Moriah is also correct: suffering people ought to be cared for. They may each try to offer the other person reasons why they're right, but it will likely be to no avail. It wasn't reason that brought them to their beliefs, it was their moral intuition governed by their dominant values.[5]

But their disagreement doesn't mean that communication or persuasion between the two is impossible. Rather, it means they should communicate in a way that recognizes the role of values and intuitions. Cody and Moriah can influence each other's views in both short-term and long-term ways. In the short-term they can redirect the discussion from focusing on the other's stated reasons and instead address the root cause of the disagreement, the prioritization of their values. Cody can try to help Moriah see that while caring for others is good, it is not always an unqualified good that should trump all other values. Moriah can try to help Cody see that fairness is important but, in this instance, should take a back seat to care. In short, each can try to persuade the other that in this specific instance their most cherished value is being misapplied.

In the long-term Cody and Moriah can help each other reprioritize their values by exposing each other to individuals who don't share their values. There is an undeniable social component to how we prioritize our values. For example,

Cody can help Moriah reevaluate her low esteem of fairness by having her meet and interact socially with affable individuals who prioritize fairness. If Moriah likes these individuals, she might be inclined to elevate fairness within her hierarchy of values. The company we keep influences the way we prioritize our values.[6]

A Case Study

To illustrate what we've said about the role values play in who we are, allow us to introduce you to a character who shows how self-discovery can lead to a deconstruction of the old self and the birth of a new one.

Arguably the most important character in the *Star Wars* saga is Anakin Skywalker, also known as Darth Vader. We first meet Anakin as a nine-year-old robotics prodigy in *The Phantom Menace.* Jedi Masters Qui-Gon Jinn and Obi-Wan Kenobi, along with Queen Padmé Amidala, land on Anakin's planet of Tatooine in need of a part for their damaged ship. While there, the Jedi cross paths with Anakin and recognize how strong the Force is in him. Convinced that he could be the one prophesied to bring balance to the Force and peace to the galaxy, they convince Anakin's mother to allow him to go with them to meet the Jedi council. She agrees, and the galaxy will be forever changed because of her decision. Over the next ten years, Qui-Gon Jinn and Obi-Wan Kenobi train Anakin. He is thoroughly indoctrinated into the way of the Jedi, which is written in the Jedi Code. The Code, among other things, calls all Jedi to resist anger, to never take revenge, to not kill unarmed opponents, and to abstain from emotional attachments to others. The reasoning behind each of the prohibitions is that anger, revenge, and emotional attachment can lead to the dark side of the Force. Wanting to become a Jedi Master, Anakin adopts these values as his own. He lives according to the Code, and he teaches Ahsoka, his protégé, to do the same. Anakin is fully committed to becoming a Jedi Master. He buys into the entire program. But then something happens: he grows up.

Throughout the first three episodes of the *Star Wars* saga, we get hints that something is awry with Anakin. On the one hand, he's becoming a respected Jedi Knight. He protects Queen Amidala, fights the bad guys, and continues his training to become a Jedi Master. On the other hand, we get glimpses that, deep down, Anakin might not really be who he appears. Although he seems committed to the values of the Jedi, eventually his real values are revealed, both to the audience and to himself. Even though he affirms humility, restraint, being measured, and abiding by nonnegotiable principles, he is brash and impulsive and bends the rules to suit his purposes.

For example, he ignores the Jedi law not to pursue romantic relationships and secretly marries Amidala. This choice leads him to turn to the dark side. Upon hearing of his mother's capture by Tusken Raiders, Anakin travels to Tatooine to rescue her. But he arrives too late, and his mother dies in his arms. Flooded with rage and bent on vengeance, he slaughters the entire village of Tusken Raiders, including women and children. Given his frustration with the Jedi council's unwillingness to promote him from a Jedi Knight to a Jedi Master, alongside his desire for power and personal expression, he aligns himself with Darth Sidious, the personification of the dark side of the Force. Darth Sidious welcomes him to the dark side and renames him as one of the greatest villains in cinematic history: Darth Vader.

Anakin Skywalker's story captures the journey of many Christians who deconstruct their faith. They're trained into a way of life and given a set of values that they adopt and try to live in accordance with. They believe them on one level.

They reject them on another. Like Anakin, they live in tension. Eventually, something spurs them to self-realization. They see clearly that the Jedi Code they once were fully invested in (a version of Christianity) doesn't really reflect who they are.

Now, please don't misunderstand this metaphor. In using the transformation of Anakin Skywalker to Darth Vader to understand the process of deconstruction, we aren't saying that deconstructors are morally equivalent to Darth Vader or that it leads to the dark side! Admittedly, there is a danger in deconstruction leading to deconversion as illustrated in the case of Vader. However, our point is much subtler. Rather, just as Darth Vader, in his inexperience and lack of self-knowledge, adopted the way of the Jedi, so too do young people who grow up in a Christian tradition. Like Anakin, who wanted to be a Jedi, they wanted to be followers of Jesus. They each had people who taught them what that meant, and they dutifully conformed to that set of values until they realized that their beliefs and values didn't align with those emphasized in their Christian tradition. Cue deconstruction.

Why Values Are Important

Why have we spent so much time talking about values? Here are three reasons why the topic of values matters for those deconstructing their faith.

REASON #1: THE ROOT OF DECONSTRUCTION

If you are in the midst of deconstructing what you believe, it's likely that the catalyst of your deconstruction was rooted in your values, which influence your beliefs. At some point, like Kate, you became aware of your value system and realized it's different from the one you inherited from your parents or church community.

Maybe you grew up as a Christian and were told what to believe about right and wrong. Perhaps you grew up wanting to do and believe the right things. At the same time, you probably didn't know that in some cases the view of what was "right" reflected a perspective that was grounded in values of great importance to your parents or church. Now that you've grown up, you're discovering how your values shape your beliefs and direct your life. As a result, you have been able to critically reflect on the tradition you were raised in. You realize you either weigh the values differently, or you understand the meaning of those values differently. Either way, a misalignment of values is likely at the root of your growing dissatisfaction with some of the beliefs and outlook of the Christian tradition you grew up with. Getting clarity on your values can help you better understand your own faith journey and also show charity to those in your family or church who weigh them differently.

REASON #2: READING SCRIPTURE THOUGHTFULLY

Knowing how your values shape your moral intuition can help you become aware of your tendency to read Scripture through a particular lens. One of Haidt's most revealing discoveries is how the reasoning of those who fall on the left side of the political and social spectrum almost always bottoms out at the care and harm pairing. Christians who lean left do so because they nearly always rate care and harm above the other value pairings. Consequently, this leads them to affirm interpretations that are consistent with inclusion, tolerance, and empathy, and they tend to reject those that lead to the exclusion of others, seeing exclusion as intolerant and unkind.

Practically, this means the more you value the care and harm pairing, the more you may struggle with doctrines like hell, the historic Christian understanding of sexuality, and the belief that Jesus is the only way, because these views seem to contribute, at least on the surface, to the harm (or exclusion) of others. When it comes to Jesus, you may be more disposed to his teaching about loving neighbors and the outcast and his warnings about being judgmental, and you may be tempted to downplay his claim that he didn't come to bring peace but division (Luke 12:51), that he intentionally excluded many gentiles from the initial blessings of the kingdom (Matt. 10:5–6; 15:24), and that he will condemn the unbelieving to everlasting fire (Matt. 25:41). In other words, you will be drawn to a version of Christianity that emphasizes empathy, inclusion, tolerance, and social justice. Whenever one or two values act as the only lens through which we see God and interpret the Bible, it will distort our vision of God rather than bring clarity. This is also the case for those who value tradition, loyalty, and authority above care. They will tend to see Scripture through those lenses and be inclined to interpretations that are consistent with them. Christians on the theological and political right need to be just as aware of their interpretive tendencies as those on the left. If we don't realize this tendency, instead of being formed into the image of Christ (Col. 3:10), we put ourselves in danger of forming him into our own image.

REASON #3: FINDING A COMMUNITY OF FAITH

Understanding your values can help you find a community of faith that is orthodox in belief and emphasizes the same values and perspective on following Jesus that you do. Does this mean we stop reevaluating our values? Of course not. We continue to read books from people with different values and engage people in conversation who see the world differently than we do. Our point here is simply to stay within orthodoxy and yet find a Christian community you can lock arms with for fellowship and service. We're convinced that such a community exists; it just might take time to find it. The Christian faith has much more variety than we often realize.

A Word of Caution

Let us end with a caution. In this chapter we've seen how your values play a role in rethinking your faith. You are not your parents or your church. You're an individual with your own unique perspective. There's nothing wrong with that. In fact, we praise God for that! At the same time, following Jesus is about submitting to his lordship, not about creating a self-styled religion according to our values. The Bible contains many things that may not match up with your values. In those instances, be careful about rejecting them in the name of being true to who you are. That would be like paddling on only one side of your paddleboard because it feels most natural to you. The problem with doing that is that you go around in a circle and never make any progress toward the shore. The purpose of deconstruction is not to express your individualism, it's to get to know your values and why you believe what you believe so you can shed faulty theological views and align yourself more truthfully with Jesus.

Reflection Questions

1. Did this chapter help you to discover a little bit more of who you are and what you value? How might this relate to your own faith journey?

2. Did you relate to Kate in any way? Why or why not?

3. What value and vice pairing do you tend to prioritize over others? How might that affect how you feel about the current expression of Christianity you were raised with?

4. How can knowing the values you prioritize help you read the Bible more faithfully?

5. Why is knowing your values so important in finding a Christian community to be part of?

CHAPTER 8

Babies and Bathwater

*Whenever we are tempted to despair about
the shape of American Christianity, we
should remember that Jesus never promised
the triumph of the American church. He
promised the triumph of the church.*

—RUSSELL D. MOORE

*Biblical orthodoxy without compassion
is surely the ugliest thing in the world.*

—FRANCIS SCHAEFFER

Did you know that in Britain during the 1500s most people got married in June? That's because they took their annual bath in May. By June the weather was nicer and, despite it being a month after their bath, folks still smelled pretty good. But a month without bathing is still a month, so just to be safe, brides carried a bouquet of flowers to hide their budding body odor. Back then, baths consisted of a big tub filled with hot water. The man of the house had the privilege of the nice clean water, then all the other sons and men, then the women, and finally the children—last of all the babies. By then the water was so dirty you could actually lose someone in it, hence the saying "Don't throw the baby out with the bathwater." Who knew?

Actually, nobody knew because the story we just shared with you about baths, brides, and babies is fake news.[1] That's right, it is entirely false. Its source can be traced to an internet meme that made the rounds several years ago. People in Britain in the 1500s didn't bathe only once a year, nor did they share the water in the tub. Even if they did, it's hard to imagine the water being so dirty that you could lose a baby!

Even though the story behind the popular saying "Don't throw the baby out with the bathwater" is false, the saying itself expresses a wise principle: *when you're tossing what's worthless, don't lose what's valuable.* That's good advice for anyone who's bathing babies or deconstructing their faith. When you've become disillusioned with a particular version of Christianity, it can be tempting to want to burn it all down. When you experience frustration and heartache, it can be hard to see any good in traditions, communities, and churches. Swinging the pendulum in the opposite direction is a natural reaction. But the wisdom of the proverb reminds us that in doing so, we might lose something valuable in the process.

We'd like to clarify up front that the intent of this chapter is not to convince you to adopt a particular Christian label. We aren't concerned so much about labels as we are about lordship—following Jesus as Lord. Rather, our desire is to provide you with clarity on a subject that may be closely related to why you're deconstructing. Our goal in this chapter is to help you identify the "baby" of your Christian tradition that's worth keeping in contrast to the bathwater that should be thrown out.

What Is an Evangelical?

If you're reading this book, you're likely a member of a conservative evangelical community (or at least *were* a member of one). If we're right, a growing disenchantment with "evangelicalism" may be playing a role in why you're rethinking what it means to follow Jesus. If so, we're sympathetic to your concerns. We consider ourselves evangelicals—but only when that term is properly defined. There's a lot that goes under the name of "evangelicalism" that bothers us too. Yet we believe much of that is foreign to what being evangelical has historically meant.

As philosophers we often find ourselves in conversations about some pretty abstract concepts. If you were to overhear those conversations, you'd notice that one question we commonly ask is, "What do you mean by that?" We're not trying to be argumentative jerks. We simply value clarity in communication. If people operate from different definitions of words, serious miscommunication results. For example, if we say, "These tacos are fire," and by *fire*, we mean "hot," but you understand *fire* to mean "amazing," we haven't communicated, we've *mis*communicated. True understanding can happen only when we define terms the same way.

Likewise, when those in the process of deconstruction use the word *evangelical*, we want to ask, "What do you mean by evangelical?" That term has two broad definitions. One refers to the baby and the other the bathwater. We will distinguish one as little *e* evangelicalism (the baby) and the other as big *E* Evangelicalism (the bathwater).

Little *e* Evangelicalism: The Baby

We will define little *e* evangelicalism as a historic movement within the church that is associated with people who are passionate about sharing the good news of Jesus. The word *evangelical* derives from the Greek word *euangelion*, which translates into "gospel." Originally, evangelicals were known as "Gospellers" because they were always sharing the *euangelion*, or gospel, with others and doing good in the name of Jesus. But "Gospellers" was an awkward label that, for obvious reasons, never caught on. Over time the name "evangelicals" came to replace it as the preferred term for those who prioritized sharing the gospel. This movement the evangelicals spawned came to be known as evangelical*ism*.

It's important to note that little *e* evangelicalism isn't a branch or denomination of the Christian church. Nor does it have a political affiliation. It is better understood as a social movement within the church united by a commitment to a set of beliefs and practices rather than a political philosophy. It might surprise you, but evangelicalism has been around for a long time. Its origins in Europe date back as far as three centuries, and it is now a global movement that crosses denominational and geopolitical boundaries. Today, there are believers who identify as evangelicals in almost every denomination of the Protestant church. This group of evangelicals includes Black and White, rich and poor, Democrat and Republican.

One reason evangelicalism is so diverse is because of its distinct form of spirituality that calls Christians to a deeper, personal relationship with Jesus through an intentional act of conversion. These evangelicals want people to know that being a member of a Christian church does not automatically make someone a genuine Christian. Rather, people need to have a "come to Jesus" moment where they respond to his claims as Savior and Lord. The fervor with which evangelical Christians preach that message has resulted in a worldwide spiritual awakening that has led to both personal holiness and social action.

The passion of the early evangelicals resulted in not only

the first and second Great Awakenings in the US but also the greatest missionary movement the world has ever seen. Men and women, committed to Jesus, left the comforts of home and traveled to the far ends of the earth to share the love of Christ with those who had never heard his name. Many did so at great cost to themselves. The Moravians, for example, sold themselves into slavery so they could share the gospel with African slaves in the Caribbean. Wycliffe missionaries, leaving England for the Far East, packed their belongings not in suitcases but coffins, knowing they would likely be buried on the mission field. Some, like C. T. Studd, a wealthy and famous cricketer who played for Cambridge University and England's national team, gave up his substantial fortune and fame to be a missionary in obscurity in China. Hundreds of books have been written telling of the exploits of missionaries infected with the spirit of evangelicalism who sacrificed everything, denied themselves, took up their crosses, and served God heroically. All of which resulted in millions of people worldwide becoming followers of Jesus.

It also might surprise you to know that many evangelicals weren't concerned with only the spiritual well-being of those to whom they ministered. They were also concerned about practical needs and social injustices.[2] Some evangelicals have been leaders in charitable movements such as disaster relief, ministry to the poor, and care for the homeless. The Salvation Army, one of the largest disaster-relief agencies in the US, was begun by evangelicals.[3]

This is also true worldwide. Consider a few examples. Largely because of the work of William Wilberforce and what is known as the Clapham Sect (a group of influential evangelicals), the slave trade was abolished in Great Britain in 1833. The Basel missionaries positively revolutionized the economy of Ghana by helping local families take advantage of the coffee and cocoa grown on their own lands. The American missionary James McKean helped eliminate smallpox, malaria, and leprosy from northern Thailand by bringing vaccines along with the gospel.[4] As historian Pierce Beaver notes,

> Missionaries were constantly the protectors of the native peoples against exploitation and injustice by government and companies. . . . They played a very important part in abolishing the forced labor in the Congo. They resisted blackbirding in the South Pacific. They fought fiercely for human rights in combating the opium, foot-binding, and exposure of girl babies in China. They waged war against widow-burning, infanticide, and temple prostitution in India, and above all broke the social and economic slavery of the caste system for the low and outcast peoples.[5]

For early evangelicals, there was no debate about whether they should preach the gospel or do good works. They saw preaching the gospel and doing good in Jesus's name (including addressing systemic injustices) as part and parcel of serving Jesus.

Because evangelicalism is more a particular posture of Christianity than a belief system, it doesn't have a doctrinal statement that all evangelicals must sign.[6] Then what makes an evangelical? Historian David Bebbington is credited with identifying four traits true of evangelicals throughout their history.

1. **Conversion.** It is important to have a personal relationship with Christ through conversion. No one is a Christian just because they go to church or were born into a Christian family. Salvation depends on an intentional act of repentance and placing one's faith in Jesus.

2. **Authority of Scripture.** The Bible functions as not only a supreme authority for belief and practice but also an object of affection. Bible study and memorization are highly valued as a means of spiritual growth.
3. **The person and work of Jesus.** While Jesus's life and teachings are revered and imitated, Christ's cross and the work he accomplished in his death, burial, and resurrection occupy a central and lofty place in evangelical worship.
4. **Activism.** Motivated by the love of Christ, evangelicals stress the importance of sharing the good news of Jesus and loving their neighbors. The result has been preaching the gospel to the farthest reaches of the world and doing good in the name of Christ.[7]

A love for Jesus. A desire to share him with others. A call to conversion and submission to Jesus as Lord. Recognizing and submitting to the Bible's authority as the Word of God. These beliefs resulted in great efforts to advance justice in the world. That's evangelicalism at its best! We think that's a "baby" worth keeping.

Big *E* Evangelicalism: The Bathwater

The #exvangelical hashtag has been around since 2016, earning hundreds of millions of views on various social media platforms.[8] If that doesn't tell you something troubling is going on within the Evangelical world, nothing will.

Notice in the previous sentence we switched from little *e* evangelical to big *E* Evangelical. That's because the two terms refer to different concepts, and we to need carefully distinguish them. The baby worth keeping is evangelicalism, whereas Evangelicalism is the bathwater that needs throwing out.

Many Americans today understand the word *evangelical* through a political lens. Whether Christian or not, they think of an evangelical not in terms of the characteristics listed in the previous section but as someone with a particular political agenda. Consider the example of Rob, a young man who spent most of his early adult life as a musician in an Evangelical megachurch. He said his church preached "God, country, and the Republican Party." As a teenager he said he was taught that "Jesus was definitely a Republican."[9] In our conversations with young Christians, many of whom are deconstructing, we regularly hear of their discontentment with the church for too closely aligning with American politics. They feel the church has sacrificed its soul for political power.

Many were turned off by the uncritical support for Donald Trump they witnessed from Christian leaders. These leaders did more than just vote for him, they lauded him with praise and declared him God's chosen man to restore the nation despite his blatant character flaws. In the eyes of many millennials and Gen Z Christians, these Christian leaders exchanged their principles (and *faith*, for that matter) for political power. To these younger believers, support for Trump was irreconcilable with what it means to be a follower of Jesus.

Coming of age in the 1990s, we both remember conservative Christians criticizing Democratic president Bill Clinton for his lack of character. "If he cheats on his wife, he will cheat on the country" was a common sentiment at the time. Yet when it came to Trump, many of those same leaders set character aside. But why? Either character matters or it doesn't. If leaders are concerned with character when it is convenient but not when it is *in*convenient, then something besides character is at the heart of the issue. Could it be an unhealthy desire for power?

Are we siding with those who criticize Christians who voted for Trump? No, we are making a *different* point. We believe Christians should look at the character of both candidates, thoughtfully weigh the range of issues through a biblical lens, and, given that politics involves the art of compromise, vote for the candidate they believe will advance the best policies for the US. Consider how Os Guinness approaches our current cultural moment. Guinness says that Trump wasn't the *cause* of America's current crisis, but its *consequence*. The crisis is much older, deeper, and more consequential, he says, than any president.[10] What is that crisis? According to Guinness, it involves a fundamental clash over freedom and the nature of the American experiment. Will the US embrace the view of freedom it was founded on in 1776 and preached by reformers such as Martin Luther King Jr., or embrace a progressive view of freedom more in line with the French Revolution in 1789?

Guinness has publicly criticized church leaders for saying that character mattered for a president in the 1990s but that it doesn't matter today. He is clear that Trump is not the cause of our larger cultural crisis, nor is he the solution. Rather, he views Trump's election "like a giant wrecking ball that stopped America in its tracks, and it allows space for Americans on all sides to consider where they see the republic now, and where they think it should go."[11] Is it possible for Christians to view current elections through Guinness's lens and to "hold their noses" and vote for Trump? Of course. The evangelical movement is based on theological commitments that transcend political affiliation. To refer to our example of concentric circles, political affiliation is not at the core of the Christian faith. It is not Christian dogma. Rather, it deals with vital but second- or third-level issues that Christians can (and *must*) debate.

Believe it or not, our key point here is not about the political realm. We see political idolatry on the Left *and* the Right. We see Christian Democrats *and* Christian Republicans putting more confidence in a political savior than in the ultimate Savior. Sadly, sometimes Christians put their political identity before their identity in Christ. We firmly believe Christians should enter the realm of politics and should vote through the lens of their faith, but we mourn when the church exchanges its mission of being holy and making disciples for the sake of political gain. We mourn when Christians seem to care more about winning elections than winning their neighbors to Christ.

In an article on why the church is losing the next generation, Russell Moore noted that much of the secularization of America emerges within the church rather than in our "secular culture." He said, "We now see young evangelicals walking away from evangelicalism not because they do not believe what the church teaches, but because they believe the *church itself* does not believe what the church teaches. The presenting issue in this secularization is not scientism and hedonism but disillusionment and cynicism."[12]

In other words, many young Christians do not think the Evangelical church believes the things evangelicals claim to be committed to regarding Jesus, the Bible, the need for a personal conversion to Jesus that translates into social action, and the need for evangelism. This means that many young Christians leave the church not because they reject Jesus but because they think the church itself doesn't really believe in Jesus. Many young Christians have abandoned the church because they feel it has become more committed to a particular political vision than the mission of Jesus. *This* is the concern with Evangelicalism we resonate with. Our suspicion is that you do too.

Endgame

We want to say it again to make sure it's clear: *we mourn when the Christian church loses sight of its endgame of making disciples and being the holy bride of Christ.* We mourn when the church compromises its mission for the sake of political power. One response to this hypocrisy is to abandon the church and to leave the faith. We understand why many exvangelicals have responded this way. It hurts to see the church abandon its first love. But there is another option we hope you will consider: rather than leaving the church, be a part of a movement to call the church back to its first mission. Paul's letters are filled with encouragement and warnings not to abandon the true gospel (for example, Gal. 1:6–9). Like Paul, we want to encourage you, if you still consider yourself an evangelical, to stay in the church and try to reform it from within rather than leaving the church because of its shortcomings.

Here's the bottom line. *If you are motivated to toss out the bathwater of Evangelicalism, think twice before you throw out the baby of evangelicalism.* If you are deconstructing your faith, this may be a big temptation for you. Furthermore, if you are reacting against a conservative strain of Evangelicalism, you may unwittingly become its mirror opposite. Remember, just as Evangelicalism can be more reflective of conservative political, economic, and social values disguised as the way of Jesus, deconstruction can be motivated by the desire to bring Christianity in line with one's more progressive economic, political, and social values. One person may be motivated to reject the values of the church. Another may be motivated to adopt the values of the culture. The latter is no better than the former. In your deconstruction and reconstruction, don't exchange one kind of dirty bathwater for another. Instead, try your best to find and keep the "baby" and throw out the bathwater.

Reflection Questions

1. What role does dissatisfaction with Evangelicalism play in the lives of those who deconstruct?

2. Were you aware of the history of evangelicalism and some of the good it has contributed to the world both in terms of spiritual and practical blessings? How did those details affect you?

3. Do you think it is legitimate to distinguish between little *e* evangelicalism and big *E* Evangelicalism, or are the two hopelessly intertwined? Another way of asking this is, Can a person be evangelical without being Evangelical?

4. Have you ever visited a church outside the evangelical movement? If so, what was your impression? What should we look for when seeking a church?

5. If you plan to throw out the bathwater and keep the baby, how do you figure out where the "bathwater" ends and the "baby" begins?

CHAPTER 9

Dangers to Avoid

*As a human being one has been
endowed with just enough intelligence
to be able to see clearly how utterly
inadequate that intelligence is when
confronted with what exists.*
—ALBERT EINSTEIN

Patience is the companion of Wisdom.
—AUGUSTINE

*The light obtained by setting straw men on
fire is not what we mean by illumination.*
—ADAM GOPNIK

To say that cryptocurrency is increasing in popularity would be an understatement. The digital cash that only a small number knew about a few years ago now seems to be everywhere. Celebrities from Matt Damon to Tom Brady have endorsed it. More companies accept it as payment, and major sports stadiums bear the names of crypto exchanges. Bitcoin, the most valuable of the numerous cryptocurrencies, skyrocketed in value in recent years, going from a value of $0.09 in 2010 to tens of thousands of dollars. Many who bought Bitcoin when it was worth only a few cents became multimillionaires within a few years.

Yet cryptocurrency is unlike conventional currency. Because it's digital, it's stored either on a computer hard drive or the cloud, not in a traditional bank. This has led to the loss of a lot of money by people who made some incredibly regrettable mistakes. James Howell, an IT specialist in the United Kingdom, accidently threw out his hard drive where he had 7,500 bitcoins saved. That mistake cost him over half a billion dollars! Stefan Thomas, a German programmer, forgot the password to his digital wallet and lost access to 7,002 bitcoins, valued at just under half a billion dollars. A Redditor by the screenname TheDJFC lost roughly $55 million when they electronically transferred it to the wrong digital wallet! Can you imagine losing that kind of money?

Three different but costly mistakes led to losing hundreds of millions of dollars. But those are the unique dangers that come with investing in crypto. Engaging in deconstruction has its own unique risks. Of course, they won't negatively impact your bank account, but they can negatively impact you spiritually, which matters most. In this chapter, we'll look at three dangers to avoid when deconstructing: forgetting to cultivate humility, failing to exercise patience, and creating straw men out of doctrines we don't like.

Danger One: Forgetting Humility

Once while flying on a plane, heavyweight boxing champion Muhammad Ali was approached by the flight attendant and asked to buckle his seat belt. Ali responded, "Superman doesn't need a seat belt." The flight attendant wasn't impressed. She smiled and said, "Superman doesn't need a plane either."[1] The champ was known for a lot of things, but humility wasn't one of them. Rather, what he may be best known for, aside from his boxing prowess, is how fond he was of declaring his greatness to anyone who would listen. The cry "I am the greatest!" is synonymous with his name.

Whether Ali really believed that or if it was just a persona he adopted isn't clear. What is clear is that Ali's understanding of greatness is a lot different from Jesus's understanding of greatness. For Jesus, "the greatest" wasn't the loudest, the proudest, the physically strongest, or the most accomplished. Just the opposite. In his mind, "the greatest" was the meekest, gentlest, and lowest. In other words, the *humblest*. In the gospel of Matthew, the disciples ask Jesus who will be the greatest saint in the kingdom of heaven. They probably expected to hear the name of an Old Testament hero such as Moses, David, or Isaiah. But Jesus didn't name one of Israel's great kings or even one of its most respected prophets. Instead, he called for a young child, placed the child in the midst of the disciples, and told them, "Whoever humbles himself like this child is the greatest in the kingdom of heaven" (Matt. 18:4). In the kingdom of heaven, the least is the greatest.

HUMILITY IS NEXT TO GODLINESS

We shouldn't be surprised at Jesus's high view of humility; it's how he lived and portrayed himself. When Jesus drew back the curtain to give us a glimpse of his character, he didn't remind us of his power, his knowledge, or even his divinity. Instead, he said that one of his primary characteristics was his humility: "Come to me, all you who are weary and burdened, and I will give you rest. Take my yoke upon you and learn from me, for I am gentle and humble in heart, and you will find rest for your souls" (Matt. 11:28–29 NIV).

Charles Swindoll offers an insightful comment on the significance of Jesus's self-understanding for us, his followers: "Frankly, I find it extremely significant that when Jesus lifts the veil of silence and once for all gives us a glimpse of Himself, the real stuff of His inner person, He uses *gentle* and *humble*. When we read that God the Father is committed to forming us to the image of His Son, qualities such as these are what He wants to see emerge. We are never more like Christ than when we fit into His description of Himself."[2]

If humility is one virtue that characterizes Jesus and *should* characterize his followers, it raises the question of just what humility is. The Greek word Matthew used in Matthew 11 is *tapeinos* and means lowly That might give you the impression that humility means letting people walk all over you, but that would be incorrect. Rick Warren got it right when he described humility not as thinking less of yourself but of thinking of yourself less often.[3] What Warren meant is that humility is a kind of self-forgetfulness, a correct appraisal of oneself that does not demand recognition or honor from others.

In his letter to the Philippians, Paul reminds us that although Jesus knew he was God, he didn't use that for his own advantage (Phil. 2:6). Instead, he became a servant to others even to the point of sacrificing his life for them. As a result, God has exalted him and given him a name above every other name. Jesus's humility led to his exaltation. He is the greatest because he was the humblest.

Swindoll is correct—followers of Jesus are most like him when exhibiting his chief characteristic, humility. This is true not only in our relationships with others but also in how we form our beliefs. As such, for a Christian who is deconstructing, one of the most important virtues to cultivate is intellectual humility.

CULTIVATING INTELLECTUAL HUMILITY

It's sometimes said that there's no more dangerous preacher than the one who has only one year of Bible college under their belt. Why is that? Because while they may know a lot more after one year than they did before, they don't know how much they still need to learn. This leads to preachers who may be wrong in their teaching but are convinced they're always right.

I (John) can speak with authority on this issue because I was that preacher! After one year of Bible college, I returned home to my local church with the spiritual "gift" of pointing out theological error. I had undoubtedly developed some solid theological convictions during this year, but instead of humbly recognizing how much I still needed to learn and engaging others in charitable conversation, I became quite judgmental of others who did not share my certainty. My motto was, "The Bible is clear; it says what it means, and it means what it says." Not only was I ignorant of the complexity of the issues I argued for, but I was also unaware of my own intellectual limitations. It didn't dawn on me that my convictions might be wrong. At the time, I would have agreed that I was *possibly* wrong, but I highly doubted I was *actually* wrong.

Paul was right when he said knowledge can produce pride (1 Cor. 8:1). I was living proof. What I needed was a good dose of intellectual humility. Intellectual humility is a subcategory of general humility. It relates to how we form and hold our beliefs. Specifically, it means recognizing that things we believe might be wrong and being aware of our own intellectual limitations. It involves being open to conflicting information, being willing to tolerate uncertainty, and allowing others the freedom to disagree without feeling the need to prove them wrong. It also means being curious about our blind spots and admitting when we get things wrong. Most of all, it means being more concerned about knowing the truth than being right.

The relationship between deconstruction and intellectual humility is a bit of a mixed bag. On the one hand, if you didn't already have some intellectual humility, it's unlikely you would ever have started rethinking your beliefs. In that sense, deconstructing speaks well of you. It shows you have an awareness of your limitations and want to spend time reflecting on where you might need to make changes to better follow truth.

On the other hand, what's true about a preacher with one year of Bible college can be equally true of someone going through deconstruction. It's easy to become arrogant and look down on others who hold to the ideas you have rejected or are questioning. It's easy to have disdain for those who continue to attend churches you now have problems with. We can't stress enough how important it is to diligently avoid becoming prideful as you seek a different way of following Jesus. Otherwise, you may be in danger of exchanging the chief virtue of love for the chief sin of pride (John 13:35).

It's important to recognize that our newest convictions are often our strongest convictions. We sometimes allow them to set the agenda for how we treat fellow believers. There's nothing wrong with having convictions. We ought to have them. Intellectual humility doesn't mean being wishy-washy in our beliefs. But it does require us to remember that the issues are complicated and that we're limited in our intellectual abilities. Keeping that in mind can help you *be like* Jesus as you try to determine *the way* of Jesus.

Danger Two: Forsaking Patience

Jenga is a great game. If you've played it, you know what we mean. The game starts with a tower of fifty-four wooden blocks. Each level of the tower is made up of three blocks lying side by side. The first level consists of blocks facing one direction and the next level consists of blocks perpendicularly on top of the one below. This continues until the tower is eighteen levels high. Players take turns pulling out one block from any level of the tower and placing it on the top. As the tower grows in height, it becomes more unstable. The tension and the fun increase as each block is pulled out of the tower. The game ends when the tower collapses. The last player to place their block on top without the tower collapsing wins.

Deconstruction can be like playing a game of Jenga. You start with a solid tower of faith made up of the "blocks" of your beliefs. Then, one by one, many of these blocks are pulled out of the tower and evaluated to determine if they still belong. As in Jenga, every time a piece is taken out, the tower becomes less stable and more prone to collapse. One must be careful not to pull out too many blocks at once. Yet that's one of the greatest temptations of deconstruction. There is a tendency in deconstructing to move too quickly through the dismantling process, tossing out blocks in rapid succession without replacing them. When that happens, your faith is in danger of toppling.

CRUMBLING DOWN

On May 24, 2001, nearly seven hundred revelers gathered on the third floor of the Versailles wedding hall in Jerusalem to celebrate the wedding of Keren and Assaf Dror. At 10:43 a.m., just as the dancers lifted the father of the bride on a chair, the floor beneath them suddenly gave way. In an instant, over three hundred people disappeared. The concrete floor collapsed and crashed through the floors below, leaving a massive three-story hole.[4] Twenty-three people perished and 380 were injured. Investigators immediately went to work to determine what caused the disaster. Many people suspected it was an act of terrorism. It turned out to be something much less sensational. A few weeks before the wedding, as part of a renovation project, the owners of the building removed the support columns on the second floor, but they never bothered to replace them. That left the building unstable and vulnerable. Sadly, disaster struck when seven hundred partiers danced on the unsupported third floor.

You don't need to be an engineer to know you can't remove all the support pillars without putting a building in jeopardy. A better approach would have been to remove and replace one pillar carefully and *then* move on to the next pillar. The same is true for renovating your faith. Therefore, when you remove a belief, we suggest you replace it carefully and wisely with another. Methodically analyze each of your beliefs separately rather than quickly moving from one to another. Here's our encouragement: *slow down*. Choose the doctrines and practices you want to consider and then list them in the order you want to investigate them. This takes patience. But what's the rush? If the goal is discovering truth, being careful is a virtue.

Mark would have been wise to follow this advice.

Mark was raised in a single-parent home. His father left his family when Mark was young, and Mark was raised by his mother. She loved him deeply but struggled with addiction issues that affected her parenting. Right before his thirteenth birthday, his mom became a follower of Jesus. She kicked her addiction and joined a local church. Mark followed in his mother's footsteps. He too became a Christian and started regularly attending the church's youth group. He devoured all the Bible teaching he heard during his teenage years. In the late 1990s, Mark went off to college with his luggage and his faith intact. He returned four years later with the same set of luggage but with a faith in tatters. What happened?

Mark encountered some great people in college. They were kind, smart, funny, and virtuous. Mark's new friend group consisted of a Buddhist, two atheists, and a nonpracticing Jew. For the first time in his life, Mark was forced to really think about the eternal fate of those who don't believe in Jesus. He knew the biblical answer, but now, away from his church community and in relationship with his new friends, that all seemed a bit hard to swallow. He couldn't reconcile the biblical view that God is love with the idea that God would condemn his newfound friends.

This is undoubtedly a difficult issue. We aren't critical of Mark for wrestling with it. We regularly invite our students to do so! Our concern is *how* he went about it. He began his deconstruction by removing the judgment "block," analyzing it, and then concluding it had no place in his tower of faith. But he didn't replace the judgment block with another belief.[5] He could have done so. There are different orthodox ways of understanding God's judgment that he might have replaced his original view with. Sadly, that never occurred to him because he was unaware other views existed. He wrongly assumed that his understanding of judgment was the *only* biblical view of judgment. When he rejected his personal view of judgment, he assumed there was nothing to put in its place, which left a major gap in his tower of faith.

Next, Mark pulled out the block of sin. Since sin is bound up with God's judgment, this move was inevitable and predictable. Unfortunately, the understanding of sin he was raised with was a tragic distortion of what the Bible teaches.

After brief consideration, he rejected it as well. Once again, though, Mark assumed his understanding of sin was the *only* biblical view of sin. That precluded him from searching for another block to replace it. As a result, his faith didn't have an explanation for why the world was so broken and evil. Having a faith that had no account of judgment or sin naturally led him to question the nature of Jesus's death and resurrection. In his final deconstructive move, Mark pulled out the block that represented his understanding of the person and work of Jesus. Given his rejection of judgment and sin, he naturally abandoned his belief that God punished Jesus for the sins of humanity. Just as he had failed to do previously, he didn't replace that belief with another that helped him make sense of the atonement.

And just like that, Mark's faith collapsed like the Versailles hall. Today, he no longer identifies as a Christian. His deconstruction ended in deconversion. We can't help but wonder if things might have ended differently if he had gone about the process differently—specifically, if he had been more patient, addressing one issue at a time: pulling it out, analyzing it, and putting it back or replacing it with another before moving on. Maybe his tower of faith would have been able to stand the strain. We may never know.

As you deconstruct, *please be patient*. Beliefs in the tower of faith are like Jenga blocks. They're all interrelated. Whether you realize it or not, changing one will have an impact on the others. Sure, some are more foundational than others, and changing those will have a bigger impact than changing others. Just like with a Jenga tower, the more blocks you pull out without replacing them, the more in jeopardy your tower of faith will be. The more central these beliefs are, the more vulnerable your tower of faith. So *slow down. Take your time. Think well* about how you are building your tower of faith.

Danger Three: Fighting Straw Men

On June 30, 1860, hundreds of spectators gathered at Oxford University for what proved to be a heated debate between Bishop Samuel Wilberforce and biologist Thomas Huxley. The topic of the debate was evolution. Bishop Wilberforce rejected the theory of evolution, arguing that God created all life just as it says in the book of Genesis. Huxley, known as "Darwin's Bulldog," argued against Wilberforce's understanding of the Bible and made a case in favor of Darwin's theory.

Sadly, there are no surviving transcripts of the debate. Yet by all accounts, it was a heated exchange between two eloquent combatants. The bishop's opening argument was witheringly dismissive and flamboyant and lasted nearly half an hour.[7] He condemned evolution as lacking evidence, being built on faulty assumptions, and having abysmal moral implications. Wilberforce ended his speech with a rhetorical flourish intended to ridicule Huxley and portray the silliness of evolution. Wrapping up his opening remarks, he asked Huxley if he thought he descended from apes through his grandmother or through his grandfather! Although Wilberforce may have thought he scored points with that insult, in reality, he opened the door for a devastating response by Huxley where he lampooned Wilberforce's qualifications as a bishop to evaluate scientific theories. Bishop Wilberforce should have stuck to his critique of the evidence, assumptions, and implications of evolution. In making fun of Huxley's grandparents, Wilberforce committed a debating faux pas—he attacked a *straw man*.

DON'T BEAT A STRAW MAN

A straw man fallacy occurs when a person represents their opponent's views in a distorted manner, attacks the distortion, defeats it, and then claims victory. Wilberforce's question was rooted in the view that evolution claims that humans descended from apes. But this is a distortion (a straw man) of evolution. Darwin didn't teach that humans descended from apes, but rather that apes and humans share a common ancestor. That's a *big* difference.

There is nothing wrong with analyzing beliefs that we find to be suspect. We *should* always be refining our beliefs. But we must not create a straw man of doctrines we don't like, knock it over, and then claim we have defeated the real thing. If you're going to reevaluate a belief or practice, it's imperative to have a correct understanding of it first.

Growing up in the church involves hearing countless claims about what the Bible teaches. At some point, we wonder if what we've been told is correct. This is especially true with doctrines we struggle to accept. We might ask questions like these: Does the Bible really teach that men are to lead in the family and church? Did God really pour out his wrath on Jesus when he died on the cross? Are only some people chosen to go to heaven and others condemned to hell? Does the Bible teach that the earth was created in six twenty-four-hour days?

When we struggle with something in the Bible, we tend to seek interpretations that reinforce what we *want* to believe. We consider the evidence for our desired conclusion and ignore the counterevidence. This is so common that it has a name: confirmation bias. We can be especially prone to confirmation bias if we are deconstructing our beliefs. If I don't like the doctrine of penal substitution, it's easy to find someone who has created a straw man of it by comparing it to divine child abuse. If I don't like the idea that God may predestine only some to heaven, then I can find a straw man version of the doctrine of election that makes it look ridiculous.[8] But is doing so really the best way to discover truth?

A better approach than creating a straw man is to build a steel man.

DO BUILD A STEEL MAN

A steel man argument, as you might guess, is the opposite of the straw man in that you find the best version of the view under question and aim to genuinely understand it. Usually, the best version will not be found by reading a critic of the view. It will be found in the works of those who hold the view and who advocate for it. Are you struggling with Calvinism? Then read clearly written accounts by Calvinists, not tweets by Arminians. Dislike complementarianism? Then find an articulate proponent of that view and read what they have to say, not someone with a YouTube channel and an axe to grind.[9] Have a problem with the way your denomination or local church does something? Find a person within the church who can effectively communicate the rationale for how it operates, not your like-minded best friend. Once you have found and understand the best articulation of the view, then you can begin the analysis. If you have studied a steel man position and you still find it lacking, *then* exchange it for a view you think is more biblical.

Deconstruction is about changing your mind. If you're going to change your mind by rejecting a doctrine, practice, or theological framework, you owe it to yourself and the position under question to make sure you aren't rejecting a straw man. Rejecting a straw man might feel good and allow you to move on with the process, but it won't help you develop a truthful faith. And that's what deconstruction should be aimed at, right?

On Guard

If you were a cryptocurrency millionaire and you read about the three mistakes made by the individuals at the beginning of this chapter, it's likely you would be on your guard against making those same mistakes. Not learning from their errors would be foolish. You would make sure you didn't misplace your old hard drive, you'd keep your password someplace safe, and you'd double-check the address you're transferring money to before hitting Send. There's too much at stake *not* to put protections in place. If that's true when it comes to money, then how much more should we be concerned about avoiding missteps when it comes to deconstructing our faith, something of far greater value than any kind of cryptocurrency?

Not cultivating the virtue of intellectual humility, not exercising patience, and creating straw men of positions you don't like are three dangers to avoid when deconstructing. Making these mistakes is analogous to ignoring basic paddleboarding techniques when the water gets rough. Sure, you can paddleboard without them, but utilizing them will help you stay on your board and get you to your destination more effectively than if you ignore them. These three pitfalls can lead to spiritual pride, an unstable faith, and self-deception. And unless you're on the lookout for them, they are easy mistakes to make. Pride, impatience, and self-deception are sneaky, subtle, and deeply embedded in the core of our being. Fight hard against them. Seek humility, patience, and integrity as you deconstruct. In doing so, you will find a faith of far more value than any amount of Bitcoin.

Reflection Questions

1. Which of the dangers listed in this chapter are you most vulnerable to?

2. Do you know others who have fallen prey to any of these dangers? What happened to their faith?

3. Why do you think it is so easy to build a straw man rather than a steel man? What does that tell you about our desire to believe what we want versus our desire to know the truth?

4. Why is it so hard to systematically evaluate beliefs, taking our time and doing so one by one? Do you fight this temptation? If so, how?

5. How will you go about building a steel man when you decide to reevaluate a particular doctrine?

CHAPTER 10

Back on Shore

*One doesn't discover new lands
without consenting to lose sight, for
a very long time, of the shore.*

—ANDRÉ GIDE

*Are you weary with your sorrowing?
Scarcely strength to lift an oar?
Christ with pity sees your toiling:
He is standing on the shore.*

—SADIE H. LEACH

When Sara Schulting Kranz set out on her paddleboard, the
sun was shining and the sky was clear. But nearly four miles
from shore, she suddenly found herself engulfed in fog—a fog
so thick she couldn't see more than ten feet in any direction.
She grew terrified and her senses heightened as she worried
about boats running her over, sharks attacking her, or currents
causing her to float far out to sea. In the silence of the fog, the
only thing she could detect was the water lapping on her board.

Desperate, she turned her board to find a landmark that would give her bearings, but she could see nothing but the white, billowing mist surrounding her—no mountains, no outline of the beach, none of the typical landmarks she used to guide her back to the harbor. With nothing to guide her and with no other choice, Sara began to paddle, hoping she was heading in the right direction. Then a shocking thing happened.

> Looking up for a momentary glance, I felt that I wasn't alone. I felt God's grace beside me. . . . All of a sudden, I began to see action in the water beneath me. Little whirlpools of water began taking shape surrounding my board. What is that? My heart racing, I trusted that God would send me some sign of protection, though I had no idea in what form. Continuing to power through, suddenly a dolphin appeared out of the depths of the great blue water. Swimming alongside my board, he was leaping and playing—he was guiding me towards shore, protecting me along the way.[1]

Lost in the fog, Sara needed a guide to help her get back to shore. She trusted that God would send her someone, but she never imagined it would be a dolphin! With its help, Sara made it back to shore. But she wasn't the same person she was when she left. Her experience of being lost in the fog out on the ocean profoundly changed her. How could it not? She had faced the possibility of being lost at sea and lived to tell the tale. Life hasn't looked the same since.

In chapter 1, we asked you to imagine yourself in a situation much like Sara's. We suggested that being lost in the fog, out at sea, and not knowing how to get back is a metaphor for faith deconstruction. You once had a faith you were confident of, felt comfortable in, and were content with. It gave you a sense of security, identity, and purpose. But then something happened that called everything into question. Now you're unsure what it means to be a Christian. You'd like to remain a follower of Jesus, but lost in the fog, you're not sure how to get to a version of the faith where you feel at home. In the preceding chapters, we offered what we believe is helpful guidance on how to do that. In this last chapter, we'd like to wrap things up with some words of caution and an encouragement.

Beware

1. BEWARE OF FOOLING YOURSELF

While speaking at a Christian camp in Texas, I (Sean) met a young man who identified as an atheist. I gladly took him up on his offer to hear more about his story and discuss some of his questions about God. As we sat down, he raised a plethora of objections to the faith, which he said were the reasons he rejects the idea of a God.

After we discussed his questions for a while, I wondered if something deeper was going on with him. Given the nature of his questions, I had a hard time believing these were the *main* reasons an eighteen-year-old would reject the faith of his family. With some hesitation, I said, "I could be off base, and I apologize in advance if I am, but I have a hard time believing these are the real reasons you became an atheist. Is something else going on? If so, let's talk about *that*."

Surprisingly, he acknowledged that my intuition was right. He admitted that the main reason he left his faith is that he just wanted to "have some fun for a season." He had just graduated high school and was headed to a university to join a fraternity. In his mind, Christianity would keep him from all the fun.

Our point here is not that people become atheists simply because they want to sin. While that may happen sometimes, our point is that there is often a core reason driving someone to question or reject their faith. The reasons for deconstruction can be intellectual, but they can also be moral, emotional, relational, volitional, or some combination thereof. But among the many reasons one may have for rethinking one's faith, one reason usually sits at the center.

Our encouragement is for you to do your best not to fool yourself about the main reason you are deconstructing. We realize this may seem easier said than done, but we want to encourage you to make it your goal. Be honest about the heart of your questions and address them accordingly. There are people who love you and who will walk alongside you on your journey, but their help will be limited by how honest you're willing to be.

2. BEWARE OF REJECTING FAITH FOR SHALLOW REASONS

Even though he had what he deemed a "wishy-washy" Christian upbringing, Dr. Paul Vitz became an atheist in college, continuing on through graduate school and into his early years on the faculty at New York University. Then, in his thirties, he came back to his Christian faith. In reflecting back on his experience, Vitz said his reasons for becoming an atheist were "intellectually superficial and largely without a deeply thought basis."[2] In other words, truth wasn't his primary motivation.

One reason he became an atheist was because of a certain social unease he felt being from the Midwest. Vitz wanted to be part of the glamorous, secular world, and he looked back with embarrassment at his Midwest roots, of which his Christian faith was a part. Second, he wanted to fit in with the important and influential people in his field. According to Vitz, these people shared an intense personal ambition and a rejection of faith. Vitz wrote, "In this environment, just as I had learned how to dress like a college student by putting on the right clothes, I also learned to think like a proper psychologist by putting on the right, that is, atheistic or skeptical, ideas and attitudes."[3]

The final point on Vitz's list of superficial reasons, which he considered the most important, was personal convenience. Vitz concluded, "The fact is, it is quite inconvenient to be a serious believer in today's powerful neo-pagan world. I would have to give up many pleasures, some money and a good deal of time. I didn't have enough pleasures, I didn't have enough time, and I didn't have enough money to do any of that as far as I was concerned."[4] So he left his faith.

We hope the point is obvious: *there can be powerful sociological and moral reasons for rejecting faith.* Alongside this, there can be powerful reasons for deconstructing faith. We want to encourage you with the same advice Sean's father gave him: make truth your highest pursuit. Don't give up the faith just because it is inconvenient. Don't give it up if you find it embarrassing. Be committed to follow truth, even if it is costly. As Jesus said, "What will it profit a man if he gains the whole world and forfeits his soul? Or what shall a man give in return for his soul?" (Matt. 16:26).

3. Beware the Temptation to Go Alone

A few years ago, I (Sean) had coffee with a former student of mine who had become an atheist. While in college, he started having questions about his faith and decided to watch some debates and lectures and read books on various sides of the God debate. He ended up rejecting the faith of his parents and becoming an atheist.

After a couple of great discussions over coffee, it was clear that he was settled in his atheist beliefs, so I left him with this: "If you ever come to the point of questioning your atheist beliefs, will you let me be part of the conversation? Will you promise me that you won't do it alone again?" He graciously agreed. I wasn't going to lecture him. I certainly wasn't looking for an argument. Regardless of where he ultimately lands, I just want to be an encouraging guide along the way. You too can benefit from guides in your life.

There is danger in trying to figure out the big questions of life alone, and there's danger in deconstructing faith alone too. We need people to listen to us. We need people to encourage us, question us, guide us, and challenge us. We are honored that you have read this book and allowed us to be guides on your journey, but will you hear the same counsel I gave to my student? Whether you are questioning your faith or trying to figure out how to land back on the shores of Christianity, *please don't go alone.* Find a guide along the way.

4. BEWARE OF ANGER BECOMING BITTERNESS

Because the desire to deconstruct can be, and often is, caused by hurts from fellow Christians, the process can easily be fueled by anger, which if not dealt with can result in bitterness. Be on guard against bitterness taking root in your life. Without question, there are things that should make us angry. When Christian leaders we trust turn out to be moral hypocrites, that should make us angry. When fellow Christians slander our good name by spreading false gossip about us, we are justified in feeling upset. Or when church leadership has been spiritually abusive to the flock, it should get our ire up. In short, sin should make us angry. Righteous indignation is a real thing. But if anger isn't dealt with appropriately, it will turn into bitterness.[5] Bitterness takes root when we harbor hostility and resentfulness toward whoever hurt us. However, it's important not to let that anger turn into bitterness for three reasons.

First, because doing so ends up hurting you. Harboring

bitter feelings toward a person or group doesn't hurt them, it only hurts you! It bruises your soul and you're the one doing the bruising, which of course makes no sense. Deconstructing because you've been hurt by others shouldn't result in hurting yourself more.

Second, bitterness can be a precursor to the deconversion of others. The author of Hebrews put it this way: "See to it that no one falls short of the grace of God and that no bitter root grows up to cause trouble and defile many" (Heb. 12:15 NIV). The bitter root referred to in this verse can refer to someone who identifies as a Christian but who, because of their unresolved anger and hostility, causes others to fall away from the faith. How so? By complaining, causing problems, and being motivated by a desire to hurt the church community that hurt them. We trust that you don't want to be that person.

Third, a deconstruction driven by bitterness never ends with a more wholesome, authentic faith. A deconstruction born out of righteous anger is one thing, but one fueled by bitterness is another thing altogether. If hurt and bitterness are the driving factors in your deconstruction, it likely won't produce a new, healthy, alternative Christian vision for your life. On the contrary, it will likely result in you choosing the nuclear option and burning the entire house of faith to the ground.

Be Encouraged

We want to leave you with a final word of encouragement. When you're lost in the fog in the middle of a deconstruction, it may not feel like it, but *there is hope*. There's a great deal of diversity within the church of Jesus Christ, and that's good news because it means there's a community of faith where you can feel at home.

What's more, there's a community on the shore that needs you. You possess unique perspectives, skills, and spiritual gifts that God has equipped you with. Don't keep those to yourself. Find a church that's within the broad parameters of orthodoxy, reflects your values, and lines up with what you believe the Bible teaches, and get involved. You have an important role to play in God's kingdom that no one else can.

It might take some paddling to find the right community to be supported by and to serve, but don't give up, because you're not in this alone. Jesus is deeply committed to you and your return to shore. He's with you with every stroke of the paddle.

Reflection Questions

1. Why is it so easy to deceive ourselves about why we do what we do? Can you think of a time when you deceived yourself about something? What was the result?

2. In this chapter we cautioned against giving up the faith just because it is inconvenient or because you find it embarrassing. Ask yourself, "Could either of those reasons be playing a role in my journey?" If they are, what will you do about it?

3. Who are you in genuine dialogue with about your faith? If your answer is "no one," do you think that is a good idea? Can you think of anyone you might engage?

4. On a scale from one to ten, with one being never to ten being always, how often do you think deconstruction is fueled by anger and bitterness? If that is what motivates some people, how should we respond?

5. If you are in the process of deconstruction, do you believe Jesus is deeply committed to you and wants you to return to the shore of Christian commitment?

Appendix: Creeds

The Apostles' Creed

Although it is named the Apostles' Creed, it is unlikely that it was written by the apostles themselves. Rather, it was probably written by Christians in Rome in the late second century as a statement of faith to be affirmed at a believer's baptism.[1] For almost two millennia the Apostles' Creed has served as the standard for what constitutes essential Christian belief.

I believe in God the Father almighty, maker of
    heaven and earth;
and in Jesus Christ his only Son our Lord,
who was conceived of the Holy Spirit, born of the
    Virgin Mary,
suffered under Pontius Pilate, was crucified, dead
    and buried:
he descended into hell; the third day he rose again
    from the dead;
he ascended into heaven, and sitteth on the right
    hand of God the Father almighty;
from thence he shall come to judge the quick and
    the dead.

> I believe in the Holy Spirit;
> the holy catholic church; the communion of saints;
>   forgiveness of sins;
> the resurrection of the body,
> and the life everlasting.[2]

The Nicene Creed

In AD 325 Emperor Constantine convened a meeting of bishops to deal with the controversial teaching of a presbyter by the name of Arius. Arius taught that Jesus was a created being who was like God, but who was not God. The bishops condemned Arius as a heretic and formulated the Nicene Creed in response to his error. Like the Apostles' Creed, it identifies the essential beliefs of the Christian faith. But it also expands on the Apostles' Creed by making explicit what Christians have always believed about Jesus, which is that Jesus of Nazareth is more than just a man. He is both fully human and fully divine. Belief in Jesus is an essential Christian dogma. While a person can be ignorant that Jesus is divine and still be a Christian, it is questionable whether a person can knowingly deny that Jesus is divine and still be a Christian.

> I believe in one God, the Father Almighty, Maker
>   of heaven and earth, and of all things visible and
>   invisible.
>
> And in one Lord Jesus Christ, the only-begotten Son
>   of God, begotten of the Father before all worlds;
>   God of God, Light of Light, very God of very

God; begotten, not made, being of one substance
with the Father, by whom all things were made.
Who, for us men and for our salvation, came
down from heaven, and was incarnate by the Holy
Spirit of the virgin Mary, and was made man; and
was crucified also for us under Pontius Pilate;
He suffered and was buried; and the third day
He rose again, according to the Scriptures; and
ascended into heaven, and sits on the right hand of
the Father; and He shall come again, with glory, to
judge the quick and the dead; whose kingdom shall
have no end.

And I believe in the Holy Ghost, the Lord and Giver
of Life; who proceeds from the Father and the
Son; who with the Father and the Son together is
worshipped and glorified; who spoke by the prophets. And I believe in one holy catholic and apostolic
Church.[3] I acknowledge one baptism for the remis-
sion of sins; and I look for the resurrection of the
dead, and the life of the world to come.

Amen.[4]

Acknowledgments

Our thanks to a number of people who made this book possible. We appreciate Mark Sweeney for his guidance and encouragement. Thanks to the professional and enthusiastic team at Zondervan. In particular, we thank Ryan Pazdur for believing in this book and for his vision to see it come to fruition. And Kim Tanner, you are one of the most thoughtful and careful editors we have ever worked with. And thanks to Dana Dill for his excellent edits and feedback on an early draft of this book. John would like to thank his wife, Nancy, and his children, Cody and Moriah. And Sean would like to think his wife, Stephanie, and his kids, Scottie, Shauna, and Shane.

Resources

Doubt: Bobby Conway. *Doubting toward Faith: The Journey to Confident Faith.* Eugene, OR: Harvest House, 2015.

Spiritual Growth: Henri Nouwen. *The Return of the Prodigal Son: A Story of Homecoming.* Baltimore: Image, 1994.

Sexuality: Sean McDowell. *Chasing Love: Sex, Love, and Relationships in a Confused Culture.* Nashville: B&H, 2020

Hermeneutics: Walt Russell. *Playing with Fire: How the Bible Ignites Change in Your Soul.* Carol Stream, IL: NavPress, 2000.

Church Hurt: Philip Yancey. *Church: Why Bother?* Grand Rapids: Zondervan, 2015.

Culture: Russell Moore. *Onward: Engaging the Culture without Losing the Gospel.* Nashville: B&H, 2015.

Social Issues: Thaddeus J. Williams. *Confronting Injustice without Compromising Truth: 12 Questions Christians Should Ask about Social Justice.* Grand Rapids: Zondervan Academic, 2020.

The Bible: Michael Bird. *Seven Things I Wish Christians Knew about the Bible.* Grand Rapids: Zondervan Reflective, 2021.

Old Testament Issues: Tremper Longman. *Confronting Old Testament Controversies: Pressing Questions about Evolution, Sexuality, History, and Violence.* Grand Rapids: Baker, 2019.

Deconversion: John Marriott and Shawn Wicks. *Before You Go: Hidden Factors in Faith Loss.* Abilene, TX: Leafwood, 2022.

History of Thought: James K. A. Smith. *How Not to Be Secular: Reading Charles Taylor.* Grand Rapids: Eerdmans, 2014.

Notes

INTRODUCTION

1. Pinetops Foundation, *The Great Opportunity: The American Church in 2050* (2018), 9, https://cdn2.hubspot.net/hubfs /4245467/The%20Great%20Opportunity.pdf.
2. *America's Changing Religious Landscape*, Pew Research Center, May 15, 2015, https://www.pewresearch.org/religion /2015/05/12/chapter-2-religious-switching-and-intermarriage/.
3. In a later section, we will address the difference between the common usage of the term *deconstruction* and the philosophical and literary theory of deconstruction.
4. To be sure, some Christians do engage in deconstruction as a means to justify leaving the faith. Our point is that rethinking one's faith isn't always or necessarily an act of disloyalty to the Lord Jesus.
5. This is not an accurate reflection of the doctrines of election and predestination. But at the time it seemed that way.
6. Michelle Panchuk, "An Evangelical Philosopher and an Exvangelical Walk into a Coffee Shop," *Christian Scholar's Review*, July 22, 2022, https://christianscholars.com /an-evangelical-philosopher-and-an-exvangelical-walk -into-a-coffee-shop/.

1. A "text" can be a concept such as beauty, a book like *Hamlet,* an ideology such as Marxism, or a religion like Christianity. Any interpretation of a concept, text ideology, or religion that says it is *the* correct and final word on the matter, according to Derrida, ought to be deconstructed because such claims are unwarranted and oppressive.

2. A major assumption Derrida rejected is what he called "logocentrism," which holds that there is a stable ground for knowledge which reason can discover. Derrida also argued that Western thought is captive to binary thinking. He then tried to show how binaries always are incoherent. The combined effect of Derrida's views undermines rationality and the ability to have true knowledge about reality.

3. We believe only the biblical narrative provides the means to build a society that is truly righteous and just.

4. For example, relativism leads to the conclusion that since there is no correct interpretation about reality, then all moral claims are not only false but equally false. But do we really want to say the moral views of Mother Teresa and that of the Nazis are not only wrong but that Mother Teresa's moral compass was no better than Hitler's?

5. Kevin J. Vanhoozer, *Is There a Meaning in This Text? The Bible, the Reader, and the Morality of Literary Knowledge* (Grand Rapids: Zondervan, 2009), 86.

6. Tyler Huckabee, "Skillet's John Cooper: It's Time to 'Declare War against This Deconstruction Christian Movement,'" *Relevant Magazine,* February 9, 2022, https://relevantmagazine .com/current/skillets-john-cooper-its-time-to-declare-war -against-this-deconstruction-christian-movement/.

7. Peter Schuurman, "Deconstructing Faith, Growing Up in Christ," *Faith Today,* October 2, 2021, https://www.faithtoday .ca/Magazines/2021-Sept-Oct/Deconstructing-Faith-Growing -Up-In-Christ.

8. We are aware of the view that having a predetermined goal toward which deconstruction is directed (an expression of the historic Christian faith) may be seen by some as a poorly veiled attempt to control others by telling them what to believe in order to maintain our own control and power within the church. To that we offer the following three responses. (1) To the best of our ability to discern them, our motives are pure. We only seek to help followers of Jesus maintain faithfulness to him as best as we understand it. He must increase, we must decrease. Our understanding of faithfulness is not our own. Rather, it's shaped by what the Christian church has always affirmed. Our authority is not in ourselves but in the historic Christian creeds that the church universal has affirmed as boundary markers of authentic Christian belief. (2) The complaint of seeking to control others to maintain our power is a two-edged sword that is just as applicable to those who advocate for, and offer guidance on, more radical forms of deconstruction. What are their motives? Does advocating for radical deconstruction increase their power by winning more converts to their view? (3) The objection rests on the assumption that knowledge claims are nothing more than power grabs (power/knowledge for you Foucault fans), and thus immoral. But that assumption in turn rests on the belief that knowledge of reality is unobtainable. Therefore, all knowledge claims are *in principle* nothing more than social constructs crafted by those in power to advance their agendas (even if they are unaware of it). We reject the notion that truth cannot be known. Therefore, we reject the conclusion that all claims to knowledge are inherently oppressive power grabs. We think truth can be known (with certain qualifications), and dialogue and debate can bring us into contact with it. We do not deny that claims to knowledge can and have been used in immoral ways to benefit those in power. We stand against that and maintain that when it happens, it ought to be deconstructed.

1. Mark Gregory Karris, *Religious Refugees: (De)Constructing toward Spiritual and Emotional Healing* (Orange, CA: Quoir, 2020), 85.

2. Here are just a few: Mark Driscoll, James MacDonald, Bill Hybels, Ravi Zacharias, and Brian Houston. Sadly, a simple Google search will reveal many more.

3. The Greek word *katalyma* that is translated as "inn" in Luke 2:7 is not the usual Greek word for hotel. Rather, it is better translated as "guest chamber," as it is in Luke 22:11 in reference to the Upper Room where Jesus ate the Last Supper with his disciples. In the parable of the Good Samaritan where a hotel is clearly in view, the word translated as "inn" is *pandocheion*, the common Greek word used for hotel. For more on this see, Craig S. Keener, *The IVP Bible Background Commentary: New Testament*, 194; Ben Witherington, "No Inn in the Room," *Ben Witherington* (blog), December 9, 2007, http://benwitherington.blogspot.com/2007/12/no-inn-in-room -christmas-sermon-on-lk_09.html.

4. It needs to be said that doing so will have a ripple effect throughout the rest of one's theology that will likely impact primary beliefs. Adopting theistic evolution will force one to rethink what it means for humans to be made in the image of God, the historical Adam and Eve, the relationship between sin and death, and a number of other matters.

5. Sam Hailes, "Bart Campolo Says Progressive Christians Turn into Atheists. Maybe He's Right," *Premier Christianity*, September 24, 2017, https://www.premierchristianity.com /home/bart-campolo-says-progressive-christians-turn-into -atheists-maybe-hes-right/3759.article.

6. Tony Campolo and Bart Campolo, *Why I Left, Why I Stayed: Conversations on Christianity between an Evangelical Father and His Humanist Son* (San Francisco, CA: HarperOne, 2018), 15–16.

7. Sam Hailes, "Bart Campolo Says Progressive Christians

Turn into Atheists: Maybe He's Right," *Premier Christianity*, September 25, 2017, https://www.premierchristianity.com /home/bart-campolo-says-progressive-christians-turn-into -atheists-maybe-hes-right/3759.article.

8. Hailes, "Bart Campolo Says."
9. Campolo and Campolo, *Why I Left, Why I Stayed*, 16.
10. Hailes, "Bart Campolo Says."
11. Campolo and Campolo, *Why I Left, Why I Stayed*, 15.
12. If you want to hear me (Sean) in a friendly debate with Bart, check out our discussion: "Bart Campolo & Sean McDowell: Why Bart Lost His Faith, Why Sean Kept His," *Unbelievable?* radio, Premier Christian Radio, April 7, 2018, https://www .premierchristianradio.com/Shows/Saturday/Unbelievable /Episodes/Unbelievable-Bart-Campolo-Sean-McDowell-Why -Bart-lost-his-faith-why-Sean-kept-his.
13. Harold O. J. Brown, *Heresies: Heresy and Orthodoxy in the History of the Church* (Peabody, MA: Hendrickson, 1984), 61.
14. Justin S. Holcomb, *Know the Heretics* (Grand Rapids: Zondervan, 2014).
15. Holcomb, *Know the Heretics*, 2104.

Chapter 3: Who Do You Say That I Am?

1. *Merriam-Webster*, s.v. "Christianity," accessed November 23, 2022, https://www.merriam-webster.com/dictionary/ Christianity.

Chapter 4: Fences

1. For an explanation and defense of essential Christian doctrine, see Norman L. Geisler, "The Essential Doctrines of the Christian Faith" (Part Two), *Christian Research Journal* 28, no. 26 (2005): https://www.equip.org/article/the-essential -doctrines-of-the-christian-faith-part-two/.
2. Avery Cardinal Dulles, "The Orthodox Imperative: Avery Cardinal Dulles," *First Things*, August 1, 2006, https://www .firstthings.com/article/2006/08/the-orthodox-imperative.

3. Michael F. Bird, *What Christians Ought to Believe: An Introduction to Christian Doctrine through the Apostles' Creed* (Grand Rapids: Zondervan, 2016).

4. Bird, *What Christians Ought to Believe*, 24, 34.

5. Of the three creeds, the Eastern Orthodox Church officially accepts the Nicene Creed, affirms the content of the Apostles' Creed, and with one minor exception the content of the Athanasian Creed. The Western Churches—Roman Catholic and Protestant—officially accept all three creeds. See the appendix for the Apostles' and Nicene Creeds. Here is a link to the Athanasian Creed, https://www.ccel.org/creeds /athanasian.creed.html.

6. Lewis Carroll, *Through the Looking Glass: And What Alice Found There* (Philadelphia: Henry Altemus Company, 1897), 123.

7. Carroll, *Through the Looking Glass*, 123.

8. Merriam-Webster, s.v. "dog (*n.*)," accessed May 13, 2022, https://www.merriam-webster.com/dictionary/dog. We have one qualification for using this quote: technically, being carnivorous is not essential to being a dog. If a dog ate only plants, it would still be a dog. Therefore, being carnivorous wouldn't be essential, but accidental.

9. Some readers will recognize this as what is known as an essentialist position on language. We are aware that the philosophy of language and how words convey meaning are much more complicated than we have presented. We are also aware that identifying the exact set of essential characteristics of a thing is incredibly difficult. However, as essentialists, we are committed to the belief that such a set exists. When it comes to the word *Christian*, the rule of faith and the creeds of the undivided church act as guides for such a set. A person doesn't need to affirm all the beliefs in the creeds to be saved. But a person who is capable of understanding the creedal statements and rejects them cannot be meaningfully considered Christian in their theology.

10. Roger E. Olson, *The Mosaic of Christian Belief: Twenty Centuries of Unity and Diversity* (Downers Grove, IL: IVP Academic, 2016).

11. Olson, *The Mosaic of Christian Belief*, 2016.

12. While most of the positions presented in the book fall within the range of traditional Christian doctrine, the position affirming homosexuality behavior and practice as morally acceptable does not.

13. Bonnie Kristian, *A Flexible Faith: Rethinking What It Means to Follow Jesus Today* (New York: Faith Words, 2018), 8.

14. See appendix for the creeds of the early church.

CHAPTER 5: SAYS WHO?

1. We believe our historic / progressive distinction captures the general contours of the two most common ways of understanding the nature of Scripture. That being said, there are a variety of what we are calling "progressive views" that address the relationship of the inspiration, veracity, and authority of the Bible. Some of these are very nuanced attempts to maintain the authority of Scripture while denying that everything it teaches is accurate or even inspired. We find these nuanced views to be unpersuasive. However, addressing them would go beyond the scope of this project.

2. One step away along the spectrum from the historic view but which many Christians hold is a modified historic view. This position maintains that the Bible is entirely trustworthy as it relates to faith and practice. The difference between the modified view and the historic view is that the modified views allow for the Bible to be mistaken on minor matters that do not touch on faith and practice, such as geography and history. For example, those who hold to the modified view would be fine if the Bible was in error in Luke 2:2, when it says Quirinius was governor at the time Jesus was born. But they would not be okay with the authors of Scripture being wrong about God

commanding the Israelites to destroy the Amalekites. That would directly teach error about the character of God.

3. Total objectivity is impossible. We are both fallen and finite. The fallen aspect of us will always try to find ways to read the Bible in a way that affirms our desires. The finite aspect means we always come to the text with a host of presuppositions that are required for interpretation to begin. These will always open or close possible interpretations for us. That being said, we are responsible to do what we can to minimize these as much as we can.

4. We need to stress that believing the Bible is trustworthy in all it affirms is not the same as taking everything it says literally. For example, some believe the Bible is entirely truthful but don't think that the early chapters of Genesis are literal accounts. They would argue that the genre of Genesis 1–11 is mytho-poetic literature, meaning Genesis 1–11 speaks truthfully about events that happened in the distant past but does not do so literally, but rather literarily. Some might disagree with the idea that the genre of Genesis 1–11 is mytho-poetic literature, but it would be wrong to say that those who do take it as mytho-poetic don't believe the Bible to be entirely trustworthy. They do, they just think the Bible can speak truthfully without doing so literally.

5. Liberal Christianity has a historical tradition and theological system. See Roger Olson's *Against Liberal Theology: Putting the Brakes on Progressive Christianity* (Grand Rapids: Zondervan Reflective, 2022).

6. Facebook accessed May 13, 2022, https://www.facebook.com /colbymartinauthor/posts/6654037121304059.

7. Again, our concern here is not with *interpretations* of passages dealing with sexual ethics that we disagree with, but rather with the view of Scripture that differs from the church's historical position. We believe the Bible clearly teaches that God has designed sexual activity to be experienced between husband and wife alone in the marital covenant.

8. This is the position of liberal and neoorthodox theology.

9. This view is generally representative of some who hold to the basics of orthodox theology but are open to understanding the Bible in ways that differ from the historic position of the church as it relates to the complete truthfulness of Scripture.

10. Luke Timothy Johnson, "Homosexuality & The Church," *Commonweal*, June 11, 2007, https://www.commonwealmagazine.org/homosexuality-church-0.

11. For a complete account, see John D. Woodbridge, *Biblical Authority: Infallibility and Inerrancy in the Christian Tradition* (Grand Rapids: Zondervan, 2015).

12. Some suggest that Jesus believed that some of these events or individuals were not literal. For a response to this objection, see John William Wenham, *Christ and the Bible* (Eugene, OR: Wipf & Stock, 2009).

13. Much more could be said here. For a full treatment of Jesus's view of Scripture, see Wenham, *Christ and the Bible*, and Leon Morris, *I Believe in Revelation* (Grand Rapids: Eerdmans, 1983), 49–67.

14. We agree that Jesus is the clearest and fullest revelation of who God is and therefore should be the lens we interpret Scripture through. Jesus himself said the Scriptures testify of him. The difference is that we believe Jesus should be the lens we use to *interpret* Scripture, not *determine* what is Scripture and what isn't. Furthermore, interpreting the Bible with Jesus in mind, we need to consider the complete biblical portrait of Jesus. This includes his grace and mercy along with his acceptance of the entire Old Testament as God's word, and his teachings on God's future judgment that he will administer.

15. The flood (Matt. 24:37-39; Luke 17:27); Sodom and Gomorrah (Matt. 10:15; Luke 17:32); the law (Matt. 15:1–4), which included punishments of both stoning (Deut. 21:18–21) and maiming (Deut. 25:11–12).

16. Matthew 25:41.

17. Revelation 19:11–15 NIV.

1. Victor Hugo, *The Man Who Laughs* (Brooklyn: BibliU Press, 2019), 16.
2. Hugo's description of molding humans comes in a work of historical fiction. As such, the historicity of this account has been questioned by some. Nevertheless, the practice of disforming children for sport and financial gain is well documented. See John Boynton Kaiser, "The Comprachicos," *Journal of the American Institute of Criminal Law and Criminology* 4, no. 2 (July 1913), 247–64, https://www.jstor.org/stable/i247466.
3. David Foster Wallace, *This Is Water* (New York: Little, Brown and Company, 2009), 3–4.
4. James K. A. Smith, *You Are What You Love: The Spiritual Power of Habit* (Grand Rapids: Brazos, 2016).
5. The age of obligation is a term we have coined to describe the social imaginary of the first half of the twentieth century up to the 1960s.
6. Andrew Root, *Faith Formation in a Secular Age* (Grand Rapids: Baker Academic, 2017), 19.
7. Brokaw does not use the term *social imaginary*; however, what he describes is a social imaginary.
8. Tom Brokaw, *The Greatest Generation* (New York: Random House, 2010).
9. Root, *Faith Formation in a Secular Age*, 17–23.
10. Root, *Faith Formation in a Secular Age*, 19–20.
11. Root, *Faith Formation in a Secular Age*, 19.
12. It is worth noting that there are a number of differences between the two wars that also affected how Americans responded beyond just a change in the social imaginary. For example, the Japanese attack on Pearl Harbor in 1941 was a significant motivating factor in Americans "doing their duty." For many Americans the Vietnam war lacked a persuasive motivating factor to go to war.
13. Root, *Faith Formation in a Secular Age*, 20.

14. Taylor, *A Secular Age*, 473–75.

15. Taylor, *A Secular Age*, 475.

16. Another important factor is the power of modern technology (transportation, communications, medicine, etc.). Rather than our having to conform to nature, technology has allowed us to seemingly conform nature to our desires and whims and to separate ourselves from its rhythms. Thus, it creates a sense that we can conform reality to our desires (internal) rather than having to conform our lives to reality (external). Modern experiences such as communicating via screens and eating processed food further separate us from the natural world.

17. A thruple is a relationship comprised of three people.

18. "I'm Gonna Be," track 10 on Post Malone, *Hollywood's Bleeding*, Genius, accessed May 13, 2022, https://genius.com /Post-malone-im-gonna-be-lyrics.

19. Don Feder, "Marriage Is the Foundation of Social Order: World Congress of Families Caribbean Regional Conference," International Organization for the Family, July 26, 2017, https://profam.org/marriage-is-the-foundation-of-social-order -world-congress-of-families-caribbean-regional-conference/.

20. Feder, "Marriage is the Foundation."

21. Jeffrey Thayne, "A Conversation with Carl R. Trueman," *Public Square Magazine*, March 26, 2022, https://publicsquaremag.org/media-education /education/a-conversation-with-carl-r-trueman/.

22. Giles Hattersley, "Adele, Reborn: The British Icon Gets Candid about Divorce, Body Image, Romance & Her 'Self-Redemption' Record," *British Vogue*, October 7, 2021, https://www.vogue.co.uk/arts-and-lifestyle/article/adele -british-vogue-interview.

23. Abby Aguirre, "Adele Is Vogue's November Cover Star!," *Vogue*, October 7, 2021, https://www.vogue.com/article /adele-cover-november-2021.

24. Hattersley, "Adele, Reborn."

25. Christi Carras, "Demi Lovato Comes Forward as Nonbinary in

New Podcast: 'I Was Ignoring My Truth'," *Los Angeles Times*, May 19, 2021, https://www.latimes.com/entertainment-arts /music/story/2021-05-19/demi-lovato-nonbinary-genderqueer -podcast-4d.

26. Carras, "Demi Lovato Comes Forward."
27. Brett McCracken, "We Used to Ask Institutions to Form Us. Now They Must Affirm Us," The Gospel Coalition, November 19, 2020, https://www.thegospelcoalition.org /article/we-used-to-ask-institutions-to-form-us-now-they -must-affirm-us/.
28. McCracken, "We Used to Ask."
29. McCracken, "We Used to Ask," italics original.
30. Everett Piper, *Not a Daycare: The Devastating Consequences of Abandoning Truth* (Washington, DC: Regnery Faith, 2017).
31. Root, *Faith Formation in a Secular Age*, 14.
32. We are not saying that submission to all parental authorities and churches is an unqualified good. Sometimes churches and parents do place on individuals burdensome expectations that create justifiable longings to be set free. We are speaking more of the impulse implanted in us by the age of authenticity to reflexively push back against reasonable expectations and regulation to realize our own happiness.

CHAPTER 7: KNOW YOURSELF

1. *The Nanny Diaries*, directed by Shari Springer Berman and Robert Pulcini (The Weinstein Company, 2007).
2. Jonathan Haidt, *The Righteous Mind: Why Good People Are Divided by Politics and Religion* (New York: Vintage, 2013).
3. To be clear, saying that intuition determines our moral beliefs rather than strategic reasoning does not mean morality is relative. Intuition is a cognitive faculty that produces in us a belief that seems self-evident in the same way our eyesight produces in us a belief that "the car is red." Whether that belief is true or false depends on if the belief corresponds to a moral fact.

4. John Marriott and Shawn Wicks, *Before You Go: Uncovering Hidden Factors in Faith Loss* (Abilene, TX: Leafwood, 2022).

5. Even when values align, there is the possibility of disagreement. There are different notions of what each of the value terms mean. For example, does fairness mean everyone having the same opportunity to succeed or that everyone gets the same outcome? How one understands the definition of value terms will often predict where they land on the political spectrum.

6. For more on this, see Haidt, *The Righteous Mind*.

CHAPTER 8: BABIES AND BATHWATER

1. Gary Martin, "'Life in the 1500s—Folk Etymologies'—the Meaning and Origin of This Phrase," Phrasefinder, accessed May 13, 2022, https://www.phrases.org.uk/meanings/life-in -the-1500s.html.

2. We are aware of the charges that Christian missions led to colonialism and the destruction of indigenous culture. There is some truth to this charge, and it is lamentable. Missionaries did impose their culture on others in the name of Christianity. That was wrong. But we are persuaded that on balance Christian missions have done far more good over the last two hundred years than they have done harm. See also, Robert Woodberry, "The Missionary Roots of Liberal Democracy," *American Political Science Review* 106, no. 2 (May 2012): https://www.jstor.org/stable/41495078. He shows that Protestant missionaries "were a crucial catalyst initiating the development and spread of religious liberty, mass education, mass printing, newspapers, voluntary organizations, and colonial reforms, thereby creating the conditions that made stable democracy more likely."

3. Thomas S. Kidd, *Who Is an Evangelical? The History of a Movement in Crisis* (New Haven, CT: Yale University Press, 2019), 152–53.

4. John Stott, *Involvement: Being a Responsible Christian in a Non-Christian Society* (Old Tappan, NJ: Revell, 1984, 1985).

5. Cited in Stott, *Involvement*, 24.
6. Evangelicalism is not merely a posture. It affirms the doctrines of historic Christianity. Bebbington's four traits identify a belief system, albeit informal and limited in scope.
7. Bruce Hindmarsh, "What Is Evangelicalism?" ChristianityToday .com, March 14, 2018, https://www.christianitytoday.com/ct /2018/march-web-only/what-is-evangelicalism.html.
8. Blake Chastain, "Evangelicals: You're Still Not Really Listening to What Exvangelicals Are Saying," Religion News Service, August 30, 2021, https://religionnews.com/2021/08/28 /evangelicals-youre-still-not-really-listening-to-what -exvangelicals-are-saying/.
9. Terry Shoemaker, "Why Some Younger Evangelicals Are Leaving the Faith," The Conversation, July 15, 2021, https:// theconversation.com/why-some-younger-evangelicals-are -leaving-the-faith-164230.
10. Os Guinness, *Last Call for Liberty: How America's Genius for Freedom Has Become Its Greatest Threat* (Downers Grove, IL: InterVarsity Press, 2018), 5.
11. Guinness, *Last Call*.
12. Russell Moore, "Why the Church Is Losing the Next Generation," Moore to the Point newsletter, accessed May 30, 2022, http://createsend.com/t/r-6C1451630A966B6D2540EF 23F30FEDED, italics original.

CHAPTER 9: DANGERS TO AVOID

1. Mohammed Ali and Hana Yasmeen Ali, *Soul of a Butterfly: Reflections on Life's Journey* (New York: Simon and Schuster, 2013), 81.
2. Charles Swindoll, "A Self-Description of Jesus," Insight for Living Ministries, August 18, 2018, https://insight.org /resources/daily-devotional/individual/a-self-description -of-jesus.
3. Rick Warren, *The Purpose Driven Life: What on Earth Am I Here For?* (Grand Rapids: Zondervan, 2002), 265.

4. Suzanne Goldenberg, "Wedding Hall Collapse Kills At Least 15," *Guardian*, May 24, 2001, https://www.theguardian.com /world/2001/may/25/israel1.
5. The issue of judgment is a significant theme in the Bible. Rejecting it outright rather than adopting a more nuanced position not only has an impact on the stability of the tower, but it will have consequences on the other blocks in the tower that are conceptually related to it.
6. "The Huxley Wilberforce Debate," International Darwin Day, accessed February 1, 2023, https://darwinday.org/educate /oxforddebate/.
7. We are not saying that changing one's mind on any of the examples means one is guilty of confirmation bias. Those who hold to complementarianism, penal substitution, unconditional election, and young-earth creationism can be just as guilty of doing so as well. The issue is not *what* one believes on these issues, it is *why* one believes what they do. Is the belief the result of a search for the truth as best as we can discern, or is the belief the result of arriving at a predetermined conclusion?
8. Complementarianism is the view that men and women are equal in worth but perform different roles in the home and church.

Chapter 10: Back on Shore

1. Sara Schulting Kranz, "How I Found My Way Back When Engulfed in Fog in the Pacific Ocean," Sara Schulting Kranz, https://www.saraschultingkranz.com/how-i-found-my-way -back-when-engulfed-in-fog-on-the-pacific-ocean/.
2. Paul Vitz, "The Psychology of Atheism," in *A Place for Truth*, ed. Dallas Willard (Downers Grove, IL: InterVarsity Press, 2010), 138.
3. Vitz, "The Psychology of Atheism," 139.
4. Vitz, "The Psychology of Atheism," 139–40.
5. As hard as this is to hear, the only surefire way to stop anger from turning into bitterness is forgiveness.

Appendix

1. Michael Bird, *What Christians Ought to Believe: An Introduction to Christian Doctrine Through the Apostles' Creed* (Grand Rapids: Zondervan Academic, 2016), 221.
2. J. I. Packer, *Affirming the Apostles' Creed* (*Wheaton*: Crossway, 2008), 9.
3. The term *catholic* in both the Apostles' and Nicene creeds simply means universal and should not be confused with the Roman Catholic Church.
4. "The Nicene Creed," Zondervan Academic, accessed November 24, 2022, https://zondervanacademic.com/blog/the -nicene-creed-where-it-came-from-and-why-it-still-matters.